Loving Pedagogy Explained

*What does it mean to adopt a lov
childhood? Have you ever wondered
really mean?*

Loving Pedagogy Explained highlights the importance ⌐
a loving pedagogy and explains key terms used within this approach.
Unpicking terms like advocacy, attachment, attunement, belonging,
compassion, emotion coaching, empathy and empowerment, this book
uses practical examples and case studies to explain what it means in
practice when we adopt this approach. It also considers how we might
adopt a loving pedagogy in relation to our policies, describing this ethos
in more detail.

Divided into two parts, the first provides a brief overview of the key
terms used when describing a loving pedagogy alongside examples of
what they mean in practice. Part two looks more broadly at the ethos
of early childhood settings and unpicks various aspects of a loving
pedagogy, including: how to write a loving pedagogy policy, how a
loving pedagogy links to supporting behaviour, how we can nurture
our children through developing a loving pedagogy and staff training
and development.

Part of the *Key Concepts in Early Childhood Series*, this is essential
reading for early years practitioners and students who want to know
and understand the importance of adopting a loving pedagogy within
early childhood.

Tamsin Grimmer is an experienced consultant and trainer, a director
of Linden Learning and a Principal Lecturer at Norland College. She
is based in Wiltshire, UK. Tamsin has written several early childhood
books, including *Developing a Loving Pedagogy in the Early Years,
Nurturing Self-Regulation in Early Childhood* and *Supporting Behaviour
and Emotions in the Early Years*.

Key Concepts in Early Childhood

Series Editor: Tamsin Grimmer

This exciting new series unpicks key terms and concepts in early childhood education and shows how they relate to everyday practice. Each book focuses on a core theme and provides clear, concise definitions of key terminology alongside case studies and then explores how these link to core areas of provision.

Wellbeing Explained
Sonia Mainstone-Cotton

Loving Pedagogy Explained
Tamsin Grimmer

Early Childhood Theorists and Approaches Explained
Chloe Webster

For more information about this series, please visit: Key Concepts in Early Childhood – Book Series – Routledge & CRC Press

Loving Pedagogy Explained

Tamsin Grimmer

Routledge
Taylor & Francis Group

LONDON AND NEW YORK

Designed cover image: Dani Pasteau

First edition published 2025
by Routledge
4 Park Square, Milton Park, Abingdon, Oxon, OX14 4RN

and by Routledge
605 Third Avenue, New York, NY 10158

Routledge is an imprint of the Taylor & Francis Group, an informa business

© 2025 Tamsin Grimmer

British Library Cataloguing-in-Publication Data
A catalogue record for this book is available from the British Library

ISBN: 978-1-032-83664-5 (hbk)
ISBN: 978-1-032-83663-8 (pbk)
ISBN: 978-1-003-51052-9 (ebk)

DOI: 10.4324/9781003510529

Typeset in Optima
by Apex CoVantage, LLC

Contents

Acknowledgements

Firstly, a massive thank you to all those educators who have inspired me with their loving pedagogy. Without you, this book would not have materialised. Thank you to my family and friends, and a special mention to my mum, who, yet again, has proofread my writing and helpfully guided my thoughts.

A very special thank you to the following people and settings for sharing their loving stories and case studies and helping to exemplify love and nurture in practice, shared in alphabetical order:

Archway Children's Centre
Balham Nursery School
Christine Wagaba
Cinnamon Brow CE Primary School Nursery
Conewood Children's Centre
Constance Handley
Copplestone Primary School
Dawn Rigby
Emma Osmond
Ewa Narloch-Mattis
Gabriela Vicencio
Jane Malcom
Jane Parker
Kate Bate
Marie Sutherland
Marlis Juerging-Coles
Mita Pandya
Mountford Manor

Natasa Lazarevic
Paraskevi Seraidou
Paul Hagan
Rachael Thompson
Sadiye Tosun
Sarah Brady
Shadia Nanyonjo
Somerset Nursery School
Susan Yaffe
Thangalakshmi Ramakrishnan
Wendy Dormer
Westbourne Children's Centre
Willow Children's Centre

A note from the series editor

This book is part of a new series from Routledge, which I am thrilled to be editing. I first got the idea for this series when talking with several practitioners about the definitions of terms I used in my work around loving pedagogy. I realised it would be helpful to have an amplified dictionary unpicking the terms used and explaining what they mean and look like in practice. Then I thought, if this idea would work well for explaining a loving pedagogy, it might also work well for other topics and the idea of 'Key Concepts in Early Childhood' was formed.

This particular book, *Loving Pedagogy Explained*, was the idea that sparked this whole series and explores terms relating to loving pedagogy. It was a joy to write and gather information for – writing about terms like advocacy, forgiveness, self-compassion and unconditional love, amongst others – each page is filled with wholesome topics to explore. I have been talking to practitioners about these terms and gathering case study material to share, which has also been a blessing! It is my hope that this book will support you in the important work you do with young children on a daily basis.

Introduction

I have been positively overwhelmed by the response to my work around developing a loving pedagogy. I think many practitioners were relieved and encouraged to hear someone articulate their loving ethos, how they felt about their provision and their way of working with the children. Many practitioners hadn't come across the term *professional love*,[1,2,3] or, if they had, they wanted something that better reflected their whole ethos and perhaps felt a little less detached, and the feedback I received indicated that a loving pedagogy summed up their feelings and thoughts in this area. I have also been so encouraged and blessed to have hundreds of conversations with practitioners about how a loving pedagogy permeates their daily practice and spoken with parents who are thrilled that their settings love their children.

My own interest in pedagogical love stemmed from a couple of texts that hugely influenced my reflections in this area. Firstly, after becoming a mum, I read some work by Dr Jools Page,[2] which challenged my ideas about whether parents wanted educators to love their children, and, as a fairly new parent, I was certain that I wanted my children's educators to love my children. I also reflected upon my professional life as a practitioner, both teaching in schools and as a childminder in my own home. Did I love the children I cared for? Yes, I definitely did. I'm not sure if I would have always defined it as love, but, on reflection, once I thought about the meaning of loving someone, I realised that using the terminology of love captured both my feelings for the children and caring actions perfectly.

Secondly, I attended a parenting conference organised by *Care for the Family*[4] exploring *Love Languages*[5] where I was introduced to the book *The 5 Love Languages of Children*,[6] which identifies that there is

DOI: 10.4324/9781003510529-1

a difference between a child *being* loved and *feeling* loved. In this book, Chapman and Campbell suggest that a child may *be* loved, but if their parent doesn't speak their love language, they may not *feel* loved. Again, I reflected upon this both as a parent and early childhood practitioner and considered if the children I cared for felt loved by me. In addition, I recognised the significance of feeling loved and having a sense of belonging and wondered if, as Maslow's hierarchy of needs[7] implies, having these needs met would enable children to fulfil their potential better and learn.

Exploring these concepts led me to study again, and I began a Master's degree at the University of Chester. My sole purpose was to research love, which I focused on for my MA dissertation. My research question was *Is there a place for love in an early childhood setting?* I wrote up part of my research in an academic journal,[8] and it informed the research for my book, *Developing a Loving Pedagogy in the Early Years.*[9]

Rationale for adopting a loving pedagogy within early childhood

For those new to the concept of a loving pedagogy I will attempt to sum it up in a nutshell. A loving pedagogy is a loving, caring, nurturing approach which underpins our pedagogy, which is everything practitioners do, say and are in their settings. Thus, a loving pedagogy impacts all aspects of practice. As this image demonstrates, a loving pedagogy is like a sea surrounding everything else.

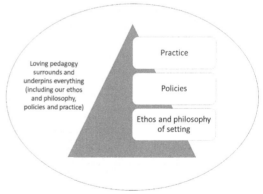

Figure 0.1 A loving pedagogy is the sea surrounding our whole practice

When practitioners love the children in their care, this results in action. They act in kind and caring ways towards children, hold them in mind and promote their best interests. I believe that this has a knock-on effect on children's learning, too, because when children feel loved, it helps them to feel safe and secure and thus more ready to learn. A loving pedagogy empowers children as they feel valued, listened to and understood. It prioritises relationships and keeps children at the heart of all aspects of provision.

Layout of the book

Part 1 of this book is designed to unpick the many terms which are used when describing a loving pedagogy. It can be dipped into as the terms are ordered alphabetically and can also be found in both the contents page and index. Each term is fully but succinctly explained, and some terms also have examples from practice which further exemplify them. Some of the examples have been written specifically for this book, and those practitioners who have contributed are named. Some have been gathered from discussions during training sessions. All settings and practitioners who contributed have been acknowledged within the acknowledgements.

In between Part 1 and Part 2 is a further reading and resources section, which is designed to support you as the reader and signpost you to additional information or resources.

Part 2 will look more broadly at the ethos of the setting/school and unpick several aspects of a loving pedagogy, including:

- The rights of the child in relation to a loving pedagogy;
- The importance of knowing what we believe – our professional identity;
- How to write a loving pedagogy policy;
- Reflecting upon our loving pedagogy;
- What adopting a loving pedagogy means in terms of relationships;
- How a loving pedagogy links to supporting behaviour;
- The implications of adopting a loving pedagogy for our safeguarding practices;
- What adopting a loving pedagogy means in terms of creating an enabling environment;
- How we can nurture our children through developing a loving pedagogy;
- How we can engage parents and work in partnership with them in relation to a loving pedagogy;
- Staff training and development.

At the end of the book, you can find any academic references referred to in parts 1 and 2. They are linked to the text throughout the book using superscript numbers.

I am using the term 'setting' very broadly in this book to encompass childminders, schools and private, voluntary and independent settings. In a similar vein, the term 'practitioner' includes all adults who work alongside children regardless of their level of qualification or experience. I am using the term 'parents' to include birth parents and also any main carers of a child, for example, grandparents, foster carers or step-parents. Unless a parent has specifically requested otherwise, children are referred to using a pseudonym or initials, and wherever possible, children have also been consulted about the use of any case study material or photographs. I have also tried to consider the representation of backgrounds, cultural heritage, settings and gender to try to ensure this book shares the perspectives of others.

I am in a privileged position in that I visit schools and settings and meet with many practitioners during the course of my work. Therefore, I have had the opportunity to hear wonderful stories from early childhood practitioners who have developed a loving pedagogy in their own settings or from students who have a keen interest in this area. I have tried to share many of these stories within this book so that their experiences can inspire others just as they have inspired me.

Who am I?

Before we start the book, I thought it appropriate to introduce myself fully! I am a white woman, aged much nearer to 50 than 40, who lives in Wiltshire, England. I have worked within the early years sector for my whole career, beginning as an early years teacher in primary schools. I have since worked as an Area SENco, advisory teacher, childminder, early years lecturer and when my own children were young, I ran several toddler groups. I have not been working directly with children over the past few years, but instead, I have been working with practitioners from preschools, nurseries, schools as well as childminders and nannies. I have written several books in relation to early childhood education, and my areas of expertise are within supporting children's behaviour and emotional development. The work that I am most proud of is my research into love, and I have used the phrase Loving

Pedagogy to describe the ethos that I regularly observe when visiting many practitioners who combine the loving and caring aspects of their role with their whole approach to working with young children. It is a joy when practitioners share their loving pedagogy with me! In addition to my work life, I have a wonderful husband and three amazing autistic teenage daughters. They continue to inspire me every day! Although, at times, life is difficult, with our faith, love and lots of cuddles from pets, we muddle through!

Explaining terms

In this section, I will be exploring key terms relating to a loving pedagogy. It is designed to be dipped into and out of as readers explore these words and phrases. The following terms will be explored:

Acknowledging feelings and
    emotions
Acceptance
Advocacy
Agency
Attachment
Attunement
Belonging and welcoming
Behaviour
Caring
Communication (including non-
    verbal)
Compassion and sympathy
Consent
Co-construction
Co-regulation
Duty of Care or "In Loco Parentis"
Emotion coaching
Empathy
Empowerment
Familiarity
Forgiveness
Generosity
Gentleness
Hold in mind

Inclusive
Independence
Joy
Kindness
Listening
Love languages (words of affirma-
    tion, quality time, gifts, touch
    and acts of service)
Nurture
Patience
Professional love
Relationship and friendship
Respect
Responsive
Safe and secure
Safeguarding
Self-compassion
Self-esteem and self-worth
Self-regulation
Touch
Unconditional love
Voice of the child
Warmth
Wellbeing

DOI: 10.4324/9781003510529-2

Acknowledging feelings and emotions

I sometimes talk to people about emotions and find they believe there are good and bad emotions or positive and negative emotions, like happiness as opposed to anger. Happiness is perceived as a good emotion, whereas anger is perceived as a bad one. However, a loving pedagogy views all emotions as acceptable and part of being human. There are no good or bad feelings in themselves, although sometimes a particular feeling can make us feel good or bad. For example, when hearing about injustice, it is perfectly natural to feel really angry about it, and feeling angry would be a legitimate response. However, feeling angry all the time may dysregulate us or make us feel bad, so channelling our anger into positive action would be a really good response. Examples of this could include doing something about the injustice, such as raising awareness, writing an email or donating money to a charity that works in that area.

Often, I hear adults tell a child, "You're Okay!" or "We're all happy here," when the child is clearly not happy; for example, they may be crying, hurt or angry. Adults must acknowledge children's feelings and also accept them, whatever those feelings are. This will validate the children's emotions. At the same time, we need to teach them appropriate ways to express their emotions when they feel a certain way. How we act or react when we are experiencing a specific emotion might be kind or hurtful, and children will need to know the difference and also actively want to choose the kind action.

How can we teach them this? Well, acknowledging a child's feelings begins with observing and noticing them, so it is linked with attunement. It is also helpful to label children's emotions as and when they express them. This is particularly important for our youngest children, who are still learning what each emotion is. We can also role-model how to respond when we feel a certain way. The song, *If you're happy*

DOI: 10.4324/9781003510529-3

and you know it, clap your hands! is a perfect example of this. It tells the children an appropriate action for a particular feeling. Some practitioners have built on this idea and added extra verses: *If you're angry and you know it, stamp your feet!* and *If you're sad and you know it, have a cuddle* . . .

So, we cannot separate our emotional side from our moral understanding, and a loving approach embraces both. It seeks to hold children's emotions and teach them right from wrong alongside feeling certain ways. If you would like to explore the process of acknowledging feelings further, you might want to look into emotion coaching, which compliments a loving pedagogy. There is a link at the end of this section.

Acceptance (see also inclusive)

Acceptance of who a child is and their individuality is part of a loving approach and linked with unconditional love. Acceptance says you can be yourself here; we value you, and we love who you are. If we imagine a newborn baby, we accept that baby and nothing the baby does or doesn't do will change that. Sometimes, as children grow older, people attach conditions to being accepted, for example, only accepting a child when they are well-behaved. However, true acceptance is unconditional.

Acceptance is also an active verb; therefore, it is a choice to accept a child. For example, acceptance says, "Although we may not want you to behave this way, we still love you and value you." We are accepting the child behind the behaviour. Although they are behaving this way in the moment, we still love them and want to understand why they are behaving in this way or what they are communicating to us so that we can support them, empathise and offer guidance for how they might behave in the future. When a child is accepted, they feel valued and welcomed. Being accepted helps to foster a sense of belonging, too. Acceptance sees differences as part of typical society, so it is being totally inclusive.

DOI: 10.4324/9781003510529-4

Advocacy (see also agency, listening and voice of the child)

Advocacy is when adults stand up for children and help them to express their views and wishes. When adults are advocates for children, they ensure that children have a say and that their voice is heard and acted upon. An example of this could be when we organise the learning environment in such a way that it enables children to access resources without their needing to ask an adult. Through listening to children, we can try to gather their views on the resources and experiences they enjoy and want more access to and can then tailor our provision accordingly. The more we do this, the more we become advocates for them, promote their needs and help their perspective be seen.

DOI: 10.4324/9781003510529-5

Agency (see also advocacy, listening and voice of the child)

Agency could be described as believing that children are competent and capable of initiating their own learning alongside enabling children to feel and believe that they can have an impact on their own lives. Offering children agency goes somewhat further than just listening to young children. It is when article 12 (children having the right to express their views in matters that affect them and have those views taken seriously) of the UN Convention on the Rights of the Child[10] is fully put into practice, rather than having lip service paid to it. It is about children recognising that they have a voice and knowing that using it may result in action, so children are active agents in their own experiences. By affording children agency, we are handing the control over to them, allowing them to be independent and empowering them to feel listened to and valued. The Australian Children's Education and Care Quality Authority[11] has written a helpful leaflet about supporting agency, which is listed in the resources section.

There are simple ways that we can offer children agency, some of which are listed:

- Listening to children and acting upon what we hear;
- Offering children choices throughout the day;
- Organising the learning environment so that children can access resources independently;
- Promoting children's independence through policy and practice;
- Believing children to be competent and trusting them to make decisions where possible;
- Encouraging children to develop self-efficacy and believe in themselves;
- Advocating for children and standing up for children's rights.

DOI: 10.4324/9781003510529-6

OFFERING CHILDREN AGENCY – A PRACTITIONER'S VIEW

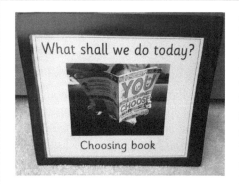

As a childminder providing care in my own home, it would be impossible to have all the resources I own out and accessible all of the time, however, I wanted my children to be able to access everything. With this in mind I have created a choice booklet which acts like a menu for my children.

It contains a picture of all the resources I have and the children can flick through the booklet and choose to play with something whether it is out or not. This allows the children to make decisions about what to play with within a session.

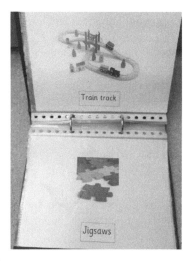

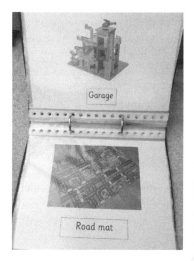

Attachment

Put simply, an attachment is a bond with another person, and attachment style refers to the way we relate to other people. Within early childhood, we tend to use the term attachment when referring to building relationships with young children. The theory of attachment was initially presented by a theorist called John Bowlby,[12] who recognised young children need to develop secure relationships with their main caregivers and that this has a positive impact on the rest of their lives. Bowlby proposed that initially, a child wants to remain close to their main carer – he described this as "proximity maintenance" – then, over time, as the child grows in confidence, they may rely on their main carer for comfort if they are worried, so use their carer as a "safe haven." As the child learns they can rely on their main carer, they build secure relationships with others and can use their relationships as a "secure base," meaning they are confident enough to explore their surroundings more or be separated from their main carer for short periods of time. Occasionally, a child will become unhappy or distressed when separated from their main carer, and attachment theory refers to this as "separation distress" or "separation anxiety." It is part of a typical secure attachment and usually passes over a short time.

There is now a wealth of research[13,14,15] that has built upon this work which highlights the importance of developing secure attachments and the way that attachments can have an impact on behaviour. Mary Ainsworth[13] further developed attachment theory by identifying attachment styles: secure, insecure-ambivalent and insecure-avoidant. Later, Main and Solomon[16] added another insecure attachment style, that of disorganised attachment. Children respond in different ways to their caregivers depending on which attachment style they have. It is helpful to be aware of attachment styles whilst seeking to build secure attachments with our children. A child can have different attachment styles

DOI: 10.4324/9781003510529-7

How can we support children with insecure attachment?

If insecure avoidant:
- Differentiation – achievable but shared interest in activities;
- Avoid face to face relating – adult to show interest in the activity rather than in child's face!
- Child needs to learn to trust – lots of opportunities to demonstrate your reliability to child;
- Child wants to be self-reliant – lots of opportunities to encourage independence as this will make child feel safe.

If insecure ambivalent:
- Attention seeking behaviour – give attention!
- If child is very dependent on adult – encourage independence with regular feedback and encouragement from adult;
- Plan for transitions as child will find these times difficult;
- Reassure child that they are not forgotten – single them out in larger group times, hold their hand!
- Bossy behaviour – offer children opportunities to be responsible, plenty of turn taking games.

If disorganised attachment:
- Early identification crucial – takes time to make a difference
- Reliable and consistent boundaries
- Continuity of care and staff looking after child essential
- Plan for all transitions, changes and differences in the day ahead of time
- Support child through any unpredictable times
- Support the emotional development of child

Figure 1.4 Supporting children with insecure attachments

with different adults. Being there and available to children, being loving and offering consistent care-giving and responses all help contribute to a secure attachment.

Some ideas of how we can build secure attachments with our children include:

- Spending time together and using positive touch with our children;
- Making eye contact with children whilst being aware that some children may not want to make eye contact, or it may not be culturally acceptable to look someone directly in the eye;
- Closely observing children, tuning into them and listening to them, responding to their needs and wants sensitively;
- Remaining calm and using a warm and friendly tone of voice;
- Being dependable, trustworthy and reliable;
- Having a consistent routine that offers structure and predictability, using visual timetables, now-next boards and objects of reference;

- Having realistic expectations of behaviour and ensuring a consistent approach (home and setting) with regular reassurance from adults;
- Allowing specific toys or comforters to help children feel secure;
- Creating a sense of belonging through a welcoming ethos, ensuring children and families are represented in displays and policies, etc.

Attunement

When we talk about attunement, we refer to being in turn with, or on the same wavelength as, a child. It is also about being in touch with each other emotionally and meeting on an emotional level. We might use the term attunement when a practitioner "let's the child know his or her emotions are met with empathy, are accepted and (if appropriate) reciprocated."[17] This would include empathising and using our body language, tone of voice and what we say to indicate we understand them and are truly listening. It relies upon our belief that children are capable of communicating their needs and wants and our ability to recognise these signals and respond appropriately. Loving attunement could be summarised as using the child's cues and signals to connect with them and engage in meaningful interactions.

Therefore, we can become attuned to children by noticing what they are doing, where they are playing, what they are playing with, who they are with and how they interact with other people and objects. We can also notice if they are making any noises, speech sounds or using talk during their play. Imagine you have watched a play episode and then find out you are going to be tested on it in the future. You would want to remember every little detail, from what the children were doing down to the colours of the resources they'd chosen and the words they used. Being attuned is noticing the detail. Reading children's body language alongside what they actually say and do, unpicking their behaviour and seeing that as another form of communication. As Julie Fisher[18] reminds us, "The effective practitioner tunes into the child rather than expecting the child to tune into them."

Ways to become more lovingly attuned to children include:

* Getting down to children's level or lower;
* Responding sensitively to children in the moment;

 DOI: 10.4324/9781003510529-8

- Fully focusing on the child and removing our agenda as much as possible;
- Closely observing and noticing their likes, dislikes, interests, etc.;
- Being curious about what children are doing and why;
- Actively listening to children and, whenever possible, acting upon this;
- Playing alongside children and co-constructing ideas;
- Recognising that children communicate and express themselves in numerous ways (100 languages);[19]
- Using a variety of methods to understand children, e.g., adopting a Mosaic Approach[20;]
- Offering interventions or provocations based on our specific and detailed knowledge of the children.

HARRY AND ANGELA – A PRACTITIONER'S VIEW

Harry was a 4-year-old diagnosed with autism. He loved playing intensely with toys but found it difficult when an adult or child joined him in his play. His key person, Angela, noticed that he loved spinning a colander filled with rice and watching the rice fly out in different directions. She sat on a table nearby with a bowl filled with rice and began lifting some in her hands and letting it sprinkle down into the bowl. Harry started to watch. She did this repeatedly, and then she added a holey-spoon and began sieving the rice with the spoon. Harry soon was so curious that he moved closer, and Angela asked if he wanted to play. He nodded but appeared unsure. Angela moved over to make space for Harry, and he sat near Angela. She pushed the bowl over to him and allowed him to explore the rice. Sharing this moment with Harry was a big achievement because, until this point, he hadn't wanted to sit alongside anyone and play, even independently. It reminded Angela of the importance of being attuned to children, noticing their interests and respecting their space.

Belonging and welcoming

When we talk about belonging within a loving pedagogy, we refer to the personal feelings of an individual where they feel accepted, valued and "at home" in the setting or provision. Maslow[7] includes love and belonging in his hierarchy of needs, and it is generally accepted that the need to belong or feel part of a community or group is a human emotional need. Belonging and feeling welcomed counters marginalisation and exclusion and should be a bi-product of adopting a loving pedagogy. When children feel loved, accepted and valued, we would hope they also feel welcome and find a sense of belonging in that situation or place.

Research investigating children's perspectives about belonging suggests that their friendships, the caring nature of their practitioners and the way they promote belonging, and children feeling like a member of the setting's community all promote a sense of belonging.[21]

Ways that we can help children to feel they belong include:

- Finding out details about them and building a relationship and secure attachment with them;
- Using positive touch and recognising that children will find physical, emotional and psychological comfort from "snuggling in";
- Displaying images of their family in our setting and ensure children see themselves and their families reflected in the environment;
- Playing music they listen to at home during the day;
- Displaying and celebrating photos of the children themselves alongside their creations – pictures they have drawn or models they have made;
- Using quotations from the children, including their words verbatim on our displays;

DOI: 10.4324/9781003510529-9

- Offering the children lots of opportunities to make decisions so that they feel part of the fabric of our setting;
- Planning ahead in relation to times of transition or change and using visual timetables or objects of reference to ensure that children develop a sense of safety and security;
- Considering belonging needs at a policy level and reflecting upon our welcoming learning environment, our partnership with families and our ethos.

CASE STUDY – PROMOTING THE CHILD'S SENSE OF BELONGING THROUGH ACCEPTING SPONTANEOUS MUSICAL BEHAVIOUR

Jane Parker, Take Art and Paul Hagan, Reception Class Teacher, Copplestone Primary School.

It is a hot day, so the reception class is in the outside area for the afternoon in continuous provision. There is a stage with a selection of tuned and untuned musical instruments, bikes and scooters, a mud kitchen, sand provision and Meccano available.

A (4-years-old) is sat on the stage with F (5-years-old). A has a chime bar and F has a maraca. A is tapping the chime bar and initially speaking to herself. F is standing next to A, shaking a maraca.

A begins to sing the first line of the chorus of Miley Cyrus'[22] *Flowers* and, at the same time, F looks at her and begins to shake the maraca to a steady beat alongside the singing.

A sings, *"yeah . . ."*

As A sings, she taps a steady accompanying beat on the chime bar as she sings whilst F shakes the maraca – matching the steady beat.

F pauses to listen and watch.

A sings the next line ending with the word "sand" and taps the chime bar to each of the syllables and embellishes the word "sand" whilst looking at F, who joins in on the maraca again – this time with a short repeating rhythmic pattern.

A continues to sing and tap along to the syllables, once again embellishing the words at the end of each line. F is standing close by, watching and continuing to shake the maraca, now switching back to a steady beat.

A finishes singing the chorus and says, *"That's done!"*

A continues to tap the chime bar to some of the syllables sung of the previously mentioned words whilst F accompanies with various short, repeated patterns on their maraca. F does this whilst walking backwards and forwards to A.

What does that tell us about A's musicality?

A is singing a familiar song to her – Miley Cyrus'[22] *Flowers*. She is accompanying herself on the chime bar and encouraging F to join in using eye contact and nodding, leading the pair of them in this musical play whilst exploring the timbre of the different instruments combined. A switches between accompanying herself with a steady beat and tapping along with the syllables of the words, whilst F also switches from improvising repeated rhythmic patterns and keeping a steady beat. Exploring the chime bar is what initially leads A to sing. This is quite common in musical play of young children. Young's[23] work supports this view "Often, playing the instrument gives the impetus for a song, usually a very familiar song, to resurface . . . . the instrumental play and the song almost always synchronise rhythmically." A is imitating the singing style with the "yeah," displaying some of the music styles that she has been exposed to. Young[24] suggests that her "Singing play reflects absorbed experiences, from home and the wider musical culture. It resurfaced to be incorporated, momentarily into her individual singing improvisation." The whole observation is multimodal, combining movement with singing and playing of instruments, which Marsh and Young[25] note is a key characteristic of musical play.

What is my role as an early years practitioner?

My role as the child's reception class teacher is to ensure that I not only spend time observing and valuing children's spontaneous musical play but also celebrate it. By sharing my observation with A's parent, I learnt what recorded music is meaningful to A and her family. I reflected on how important it is to talk to parents to find out what they and their children like to listen to. Once you know this, you could then create a class playlist based on music that is meaningful to children in your care – and play it at various times in the day, including when children arrive or leave your setting at the beginning or end of your session. I feel the influence of media and the child's family musical preferences may play a major role in their sense of belonging. Hargreaves, Marshall and North[26] suggest that listening to pop music is such a central part of teenagers' lives that it becomes a "badge of identity" for many of them. Equally, *Flowers* by Miley Cyrus could be argued as a part of A's young life and is a badge of identity for them. I highly recommend you invite parents to share what music is listened to at home. This can be powerful and – as Burke[27] suggests – it could perhaps help settle children, using music from home to provide security.

Behaviour

A loving approach to behaviour sees it as communication, recognises there is always a reason for a child's behaviour and seeks to understand the child holistically. It emphasises the importance of adopting a relational approach which puts relationships at the heart of practice and does not rely on sanctions, rewards and punishments to coerce children to conform. Instead, it actively teaches children right from wrong, helps them to develop their moral understanding and learn how to respond appropriately. In my book *Supporting Behaviour and Emotions*,[28] I suggest we need to become behaviour detectives to work out why children behave the way they do so that we can be proactive rather than reactive in our response.

Behaviour management is a term which is often used in relation to supporting children; however, this term is now outdated and unhelpful, as it implies we need to "manage" children's behaviour in an adult directive way rather than teach children how to behave in kind and caring ways. A better approach is to focus on nurturing self-regulation because

> talking about managing children's behaviour introduces a power dynamic that is both unhelpful and unnecessary. It doesn't see the child as competent but, rather, as someone needing managing. Therefore, thinking about behaviour in terms of relationships, our pedagogical approach and our role in co-regulating children is more helpful and supportive.[29]

I am currently writing a book for this series called *Behaviour Explained* which will unpick several of the terms used in relation to behaviour, so do look out for it!

DOI: 10.4324/9781003510529-10

Caring

Caring is a term we often use when we think of our loving approach. To care for someone includes looking after them, feeling a level of concern for them and considering their needs. Our industry is often called *childcare*, and caring is an essential part of our role. It could be argued that loving goes further than caring, and love and care are not terms that are synonymous with each other; however, a loving approach fully incorporates all aspects of caring.

Nell Noddings[30] has researched caring and challenged schools and educational establishments to adopt a more caring ethos. Despite this challenge, education is still often lacking in care, and care is differentiated from education. Within early childhood, the term *educare* has sometimes been used to indicate the combination of providing both education and care to children, perhaps within a childcare capacity; however, generally speaking, education is separated from care. This makes very little sense, as being an early childhood practitioner is a very caring and nurturing career!

Communication (including non-verbal)

To communicate is to exchange information with another person, either using words, signs, symbols, body language or behaviour. The world can be a frightening place when we don't understand what's going on around us or we are unable to communicate our needs. Babies, young children and some of our older children communicate very effectively without words, and practitioners who are attuned to their children usually understand them. There are many different ways that young children communicate and methods of listening to them – language is part of the story, but not the whole story. We will, of course, listen to what children actually say and how they say it; however, very young children are just learning language, and many children will find language difficult or have trouble communicating. We will, therefore, need to listen to them using other methods, and the majority of communication methods are non-verbal.

Observing children is the best place to start: observing the sounds they make, noticing their body language and how they make eye contact or what they are looking at, observing any gestures they make, perhaps they can point or use sign language. Sometimes, we can listen to our children through their pictures or drawings, but mostly, we will be listening to them through their behaviour and emotions. So consider what they do, what their interests are, where they play and how long they play there – if a child spends a long time in a certain area or with a certain resource, we can assume they like it! Notice who they play with and note any emotions the child is experiencing.

Thinking about children's communication reminds me of the beautiful poem, *The Child is made of one hundred*, by Loris Malaguzzi, shared at the start of the book *The hundred languages of children*,[19] which outlines multiple ways children express themselves and highlights their potential. Practitioners need to listen to children's languages

DOI: 10.4324/9781003510529-12

as we communicate with them. This also links with love languages[6] and the idea that children express feelings of love in different ways. We need to learn to speak out children's love languages to help them feel fully loved.

NON-VERBAL COMFORT AND CARE – A PRACTITIONER'S VIEW

Westbourne children's centre

Lucas has been settling into the baby room and is a child who has experienced severe trauma, including witnessing domestic violence. He is 18 months old. His key person is working to establish herself as his safe, secure base as he is finding it very difficult to leave his Mother. Lucas screams loudly throughout the day, and even the most skilled distraction techniques don't work for long.

Two days ago, I placed myself alongside where Lucas was standing but avoided eye contact, and manipulated a few animal toys on a countertop whilst conversing with children across the room. Lucas initially went to throw the toys. I was kneeling, and his key person moved to stand slightly behind Lucas with her feet about 30 cm apart. Lucas then moved backwards to stand almost between her legs. As soon as he felt her touch, he stopped the loud noise he was making and observed the toy movement. Neither I nor his key person spoke to him or gave him any eye contact. Receiving the physical touch from his key adult provided the security he needed to engage with the actions within the room visually. He observed the change of routine as the other children prepared to wash their hands for lunch and then took his key person's hand as she guided him to sit with her for his meal. This was a big achievement for Lucas to accept a routine change without showing any frustration.

27

Compassion and sympathy
(see also empathy)

Feeling sympathy and being compassionate are natural responses within a loving relationship. If we notice a child or family going through a difficult time, hurting or suffering in some way, we will naturally feel concerned about them. Having sympathy is feeling bad for someone if they are experiencing difficulties and being sincerely concerned for them. For example, we might be sympathetic toward a child if they fall and hurt themselves, saying, "I'm so sorry you have fallen over!" Empathy is imagining exactly how we would feel in that situation, so it takes sympathy a step further by feeling the pain, for example, saying, "Ouch, it really hurts when you fall over, doesn't it!?" Compassion takes this idea even further still because compassion is not just understanding how someone might feel and feeling sorry for them, but it includes a desire to help in the situation. We need to nurture children's feelings of sympathy and empathy and teach them how to be caring and compassionate people.

The word compassion comes from the Latin word "compati," which literally means to suffer with; although a definition of compassion goes further than just empathising with someone, it also involves action and a desire to help. According to Strauss et al.,[31] "compassion consists of five elements: recognizing suffering, understanding the universality of human suffering, feeling for the person suffering, tolerating uncomfortable feelings, and motivation to act/acting to alleviate suffering." It is generally accepted that with compassion, there is more distance between us and the person we are compassionate towards, empathising would mean we are sitting alongside someone, sometimes crying with them and saying I can imagine exactly how you feel, but with compassion, we can not only understand and empathise, but also do something to help.

DOI: 10.4324/9781003510529-13

SYMPATHY, EMPATHY AND COMPASSION EXPLAINED

Context – your friend says – "My dog has died . . ."

Sympathy says – "Oh, your poor thing, you must feel really sad."

Empathy says – "I can imagine how you are feeling. You loved your dog, and it hurts to lose a pet that you love."

Compassion says – "I know you must be feeling really sad right now, and I can empathise with you, but I also want to help. What can I do?"

Compassion acts – for example, through making a photobook containing lovely pictures of their dog, sending a sympathy card to our friend and offering to take them out for a coffee.

Consent

Touch is part and parcel of a loving pedagogy, and consent is about asking for and gaining permission from a child that they are happy to be positively touched. Many of our children are too young to give verbal consent; therefore, we need to observe their body language and notice their behaviour as well as listen to their words. We need to look out for any signs of dissent, for example, when a child looks uncomfortable or shows us that they do not want to be touched, and then ensure we listen to their views and act upon them. Teaching consent from an early age is vital because this sets the tone for life and can empower children to have autonomy over their bodies and who can and can't touch them. If children learn from birth that adults ask before touching them, it protects them from the dangerous narrative that children must always do what adults say.

We need to model consent and encourage parents to also develop a culture of consent. This can begin from birth, for example, by asking a child – "Can I change your nappy?" Or "Do you want Sarah or Linsa to change your nappy?" This is about engaging in respectful communication with children and is part and parcel of a loving pedagogy. Asking a child for consent will also involve teaching children the serve and return of conversation. For example, we might say, "I'm going to change your nappy now, is that OK?" and then wait a moment before carrying on, "Come on then, let's go to the changing table . . ." The idea is to make eye contact, acknowledge the child and include them in the process and experience rather than simply do things to them.

It's also important to remember about consent if children are meeting other adults, including family members; I've heard parents say to their children before, "Go and give Grandad a hug before we go . . ." whereas they should be asking, "Would you like to give Grandad a hug

 DOI: 10.4324/9781003510529-14

before we go?" and both Grandad and parent need to accept if the answer is no! However, as demonstrated in the case study, which reflects upon consent with family members, many adults will naturally encourage consent as part of their loving everyday interactions.

REFLECTION ON CONSENT WITH FAMILY MEMBERS

Whilst working with settings around consent, I have been reflecting back upon interactions in my own home. Although when my children were little, I had not explicitly thought about relationships in terms of consent, all members of the family always tried to listen to our children's non-verbal communication. For example, when offering to read a story, we might say, "Would you like to sit on my lap?" and allow our children to climb up voluntarily or, if they were too young, lift them onto our lap, noticing any signs of dissent. I have a wealth of lovely pictures, such as this one, which depicts my daughters happily sitting on their Grandparents' knees and listening to a story. On reflection, we were naturally encouraging consent through listening to our children and responding to their cues in a loving way.

Early childhood practitioners need to educate others and explain boundaries and consent to them. We may need to introduce this idea to parents and carers and role models, asking for consent in the presence of parents, e.g., on arrival and pick up . . . "Shall we wave goodbye or would you like a hug goodbye?"

Here are some key principles to bear in mind when considering consent:

- Establish rules about consent within early childhood and set the tone for life.
- Think about what constitutes appropriate touch (adult:child, child:child, child:adult).
- Who initiates the contact?
- Consider consent for images.
- Talk about consent with children.
- Children have a right to say no.
- Role model asking for and giving consent, e.g., "Do you need a hug?" "Yes, you can hold my hand."

Lastly, we can also teach children to ask for consent from others. Asking for consent is as simple as asking opinions, for example, "Do you want to play with the red or blue car?" sharing toys and games; "Can I play with you?" and understanding about personal space; "Can I sit next to you?" Other ways that we can ask children for consent include direct questions; for example, "Do you want a hug hello today? We could also wave or high five . . ." or "Can I sit beside you while we read this book?"

Co-construction

The term co-construction is used to describe children and children, or children and adults engaging as equal partners whilst they play and learn and help "construct" learning or knowledge together. They might be talking about what they are doing, building on each other's thoughts or bouncing ideas off each other. "Through shared activity, communication, cooperation, and even conflict, children co-construct their knowledge of the world, using one child's idea to develop another's, or to explore a path yet unexplored."[32]

Co-construction depends upon the adults and children having built secure relationships with each other, and when adults and children co-construct learning, they are usually totally immersed and engaged in the process. Co-construction is a respectful way of scaffolding and working with children, supporting their learning rather than always teaching in a very top-down or adult-controlling way. It is based on the view that children are competent and arrive in our settings with a certain amount of knowledge and experiences which we build upon.

Co-regulation (see also self-regulation and emotion coaching)

Children are still developing self-regulation and do not yet know how to deal with their powerful feelings and thoughts and, as a result, do not always know the appropriate ways to behave in specific circumstances. Part of our role as a practitioner is to help children regulate their emotions by becoming co-regulators and actively listening and being attuned to children's emotional states. Co-regulation is a supportive process when adults interact in the moment, coach and role-model to scaffold their learning. It relies on us having built a secure relationship with our children and the children feeling safe and secure with us. As well as being something we do in the moment through role-modelling appropriate responses, co-regulation builds resilience in children and also teaches them strategies they can use if they feel that same way in the future. Emotion coaching is a method of co-regulation.

We cannot co-regulate if we are stressed or upset ourselves. You will have heard of the phrase "put on your oxygen mask before helping others," and it is the same with co-regulation. If we are not self-regulated ourselves, we cannot be there for the children and offer them a calming influence through co-regulation.

ROLE MODELLING SELF-REGULATION – A CHILDMINDER'S VIEW

As part of my role as a childminder, I teach children how to respond to their emotions and try to be aware of my own. I was reminded recently of how we are always role modelling, even when we don't mean to me. For example, once, when I felt

 DOI: 10.4324/9781003510529-16

overwhelmed, instead of reacting to the behaviour I gave myself a moment away from the child. This child noticed it, so when they were overwhelmed, instead of reacting, they did what I did and took themselves away for a moment to calm down.

Duty of care or "In Loco Parentis"

Sometimes, the term "In Loco Parentis" is used to describe the duty of care that we have when working with children. This term stemmed from common law and meant practitioners should care for a child in the same way a parent would. The statutory framework for the Early Years Foundation Stage[33] in England says that providers have a "duty of care," although it does not define this further; however, the definition of this in relation to schools says, "Teachers and other staff in schools have a common law duty when in charge of pupils to take the same care of them as they would as a parent,"[34] so it is fair to also adopt this definition within early childhood.

When caring for a child in the same way as a parent, we can also reflect upon demonstrating love in the same way as a parent. For example, parents demonstrate love through:

- Physical affection: cuddles, kisses, hugs;
- Care: food, shelter, warmth;
- Emotional warmth: attachment and bonding;
- Protecting their child: health, safety;
- Promoting their interests;
- Offering guidance and boundaries;
- Holding them in mind when not with them.

As early years practitioners, depending on our role and relationship with the child, we can demonstrate our love to them in these ways, too. In *Developing a Loving Pedagogy*,[9] I refer to Alex Wood,[35] who suggests that the teacher's and parent's roles are practically identical in their desire to care for and protect children and put their interests before our own. He makes several claims about professional love which he believes apply to teachers as well as parents.

DOI: 10.4324/9781003510529-17

REFLECTION POINT

Wood's claims about professional love[35] as norms by which teachers operate

- We are committed to caring for and protecting our children.
- We will treat our children as individuals with different needs and expectations.
- We will put their interests before our own. We will seek to teach them, "by precept and example," how to live and live well.
- We will encourage them to develop as thinkers, learners, members of a family, a circle of friends, a community and society.
- We will offer them our knowledge and understanding of language, culture and society but recognise that our knowledge is limited and insufficient and they will require also to learn from others.
- We will protect their health and safety and encourage the development of their physical strength and aptitudes.
- We will attempt to guide them towards accessing life's varied experiences at appropriate levels and stages.
- We will praise their successes, support them through their failures, and encourage them to be aware that life will bring a share of both.
- Above all else, we will happily accept their short-term dependency and encourage, look forward to, and prepare them for, independence.

Read through the previous points and, taking each one in turn, think about the practical application of this claim. What does it look like in practice on a daily basis?

Emotion coaching

Emotion coaching recognises the importance of the emotions under-pinning behaviour and is an empathetic strategy. An emotion coaching approach is based on the belief that all emotions are acceptable, but some behaviours are not. Emotion coaching stems from the work of John Gottman and colleagues,[36] who noticed the way parents respond to their children's behaviour and the impact these responses had on their emotions. Many of the typical ways a parent responded ignored the world of emotions, whereas the approach which provided both empathy and support was when parents became an emotion coach. Emotion coaching is a method of co-regulation and follows a simple process of responding to the child in the moment, recognising the children's feelings and empathising, then validating them by naming or labelling them before exploring the issue further with the child. Sometimes this requires the adult to set limits, expectations or bound-aries on the behaviour to help the child understand appropriate and acceptable behaviours or problem-solve alongside them, which turns the situation into a problem and scaffolds the child in finding ways for-ward. A really helpful book about emotion coaching is called *Emotion Coaching with Children and Young People in Schools*.[37]

Figure 1.6 The steps of Emotion Coaching (Gilbert, Gus and Rose, 2021)

DOI: 10.4324/9781003510529-18

EMOTION COACHING IN PRACTICE – A PRACTITIONER'S VIEW

During a stay and play session, a 4-year-old boy, Ethan, wanted to play with a pop-up toy that 2-year-old Josh was playing with. I was in a leadership role during this session, and both children had a parent present. I was calm but also very conscious that the children's parents were watching and could hear what was going on, too. I knelt on the floor next to the children and held onto the toy to stop the tug-of-war that had ensued. I said to them, "Ethan, you look like you really want that toy. Josh you look cross because you want to keep the toy. It looks like you both really want to play with this . . ." Both children looked at me, probably wondering what I was doing. I continued, "So we have a problem; there are (counts) one, two children, and (counts) one pop-up toy. I wonder what we can do?" Ethan said, "Josh can get another one," and I replied in a slightly sad tone, "I don't think we have another one . . ." I was still holding the toy but noticed an instrument basket nearby, so I briefly let go of the pop-up toy and grabbed the basket, ensuring it made a noise as I did so. Then Ethan said, "Maybe I can have this, and Josh can have one of those . . ." He pointed to the instruments. Josh didn't say anything but was attracted by the basket that had appeared and happily started to root through the basket to choose an instrument.

Using emotion coaching with the children helped both children to think about the situation and engage with me as we talked through the issue. Ethan understood our discussion more than Josh, possibly due to Josh being only two-years-old. Ethan solved the problem and, in doing so, perhaps learned one possible way of resolving conflict for the future. The situation resolved and remained calm, and a potential conflict was averted. I had been able to role model emotion coaching and how to respond to children fighting over resources to the parents who were present.

Empathy (see also compassion)

Empathy is when we can imagine exactly how someone feels in their given situation, we put ourselves in their shoes and think how we would feel if we were them. It relies on us having had first-hand experiences of different situations and different feelings. Young children are still developing empathy, partly because they are still learning about emotions and how they make them feel. They are able to respond emotionally to someone else and the situation they are in, but they may find it difficult to imagine how they must feel in that situation. In order to be empathetic, we need to have Theory of Mind (ToM) and recognise that other people have feelings that may be different from ours, seeing the world from their perspective.

Developing empathy is part of children's social development – it is a pro-social behaviour and one we want to foster in our children; however, in order for children to develop empathy, they need to feel safe, secure and loved themselves. Young children develop empathy over many years, and it is difficult to say developmentally when all children will be able to empathise, with some studies suggesting this is well into our teens. Despite this, it is a skill that is part of our ability to self-regulate because empathy is all about understanding how our behaviour, words and actions might impact someone else, considering how they might feel and maintaining control or inhibiting our impulses.

A great way to promote empathy is to share our feelings, talk about what we are feeling and why and, in doing so, we are explaining and exemplifying that emotion. When we do this, it is helpful to highlight that we don't always know what other people are thinking or what they would like, for example, but we can find out by asking them. We also need to explain to children that sometimes other people's thoughts and feelings will be different from our own. So use the language associated with thinking and feeling, for example, "Do you remember visiting the

DOI: 10.4324/9781003510529-19

zoo and seeing the penguin eating a fish? It really made us laugh!" Talking about our thoughts, feelings and emotions in the moment and about past or future events will help children reflect on this themselves. In addition, sharing books and stories with children where we talk about how the characters are feeling or what they are doing and why will help to make an abstract thing (feelings) more concrete.

Empowerment

A loving pedagogy empowers our children. When we talk about empowering children, we mean helping them to feel more in control of their lives and that their voices will be listened to. Young children have very little power and control over their lives; adults decide where they go, when they go there, who they see, often what they wear and what they eat. When we lovingly nurture our children, we try to empower them through everyday routines and help them feel competent by offering them choices, allowing them to make decisions and following their lead within play, which allows them to gain mastery over their play.

Ways that we can help our children to feel empowered include:

- Getting down on their level when engaging with them;
- Removing the power dynamic so that we are offering them agency and journeying alongside them rather than always directing them;
- Asking for their views and opinions about things;
- Allowing them to make choices throughout the day;
- Listening to them and acting upon what they say when possible;
- Not talking to others over their heads or about them when they are present;
- Including them in our conversations in age-appropriate ways and not patronising them;
- Playing alongside them, co-creating, co-constructing learning together;
- Enabling our children by scaffolding tasks and activities;
- Supporting them to resolve conflicts and problem-solve solutions;
- Teaching them strategies they can use when adults are not available to help, e.g., breathing techniques, using zones of regulation or a visual timetable;

DOI: 10.4324/9781003510529-20

- Role modelling and offering the children words and phrases or scripts they can use to empower themselves, e.g., "Stop!," "Can I play?" and "Yes, you can hold my hand!"
- Promoting their independence and helping them to be successful in their endeavours.

HELPING OUR FRIENDS – A PRACTITIONER'S VIEW

Archway and Willow Children's Centres

In the preschool, we are embedding a loving pedagogy by encouraging the children to express their feelings and emotions. We support them in resolving their conflicts by **empowering** them, for example, in recognising their own emotions and how to express or channel them in a more positive and healthy way. One way is by encouraging the children to use breathing techniques, which are very effective

in terms of supporting them to self-regulate – especially those who are prone to emotional meltdowns. The children are also very aware of the calming area and resources and can take themselves to the calming area and often, if they see another child who is upset, they will, without any prompting from the adult, invite their friend to use the area.

The staff are very aware of the RULER strategies (Recognise, Understand, Label, Express, Regulate), and they are actively implemented throughout the day, empowering the children. The staff are equally empowered by the strategies and are more alert to triggers or any changes in the behaviours of children. When a child hurts another child, children are encouraged to say "STOP" using the Makaton sign and, if able to, also say, "I don't like it." This empowering strategy has initiated conversations about how they think their friend might be feeling, and thus, they begin to understand empathy and positive relationships. Through these strategies, the children are able to overcome most of their minor conflicts, which then gives them an injection of confidence in their interactions, alongside clear knowledge that the adults are accessible and attuned to their needs. These empowering strategies have also supported the children in forming positive relationships with their peers and helping each other.

The photo shows a little boy helping his friend with his zip while others are observing and developing an understanding of the importance of helping. Through our daily and continuous provision, we consistently promote a loving pedagogy and empower children by role-modelling it ourselves as adults.

When we are familiar with someone, we are close to them, and we know and notice things about their lives. Often, this term is used to express feeling relaxed around someone and encompasses friendliness. Familiarity is also about intimacy and, as you might guess, one origin of the word is linked with belonging to a family or household. The more familiar a child is with the other children and adults in our setting, the more they will feel they belong and are safe and secure with us.

The familiarity effect suggests that we develop preferences for things because we are familiar with them, which can help children feel at home in our setting. There is also a similar effect in relation to people, called the propinquity effect,[38] which means that we are more likely to develop friendships and close relationships with people we regularly encounter. Therefore, being familiar with others will help a child to develop relationships and is part of their social development and competence as they become acquainted with their peers and get to know the other children better over time. One way that we can do this is to use the children's names regularly, encourage the children to use each other's names, and talk to them about their likes, dislikes and interests.

LEARNING NAMES – A PRACTITIONER'S VIEW

When a visitor came to our setting, child T (4-year-old) was keen to introduce them to all the children, pointing out the children individually by name. Then he got to a couple of children whose names he didn't know, and he described them as "that one in blue" and "the little girl who likes puddles." The manager was able to tell child T the names of these children, and it highlighted to the adults the importance of using children's names and encouraging the children to learn more about each other.

DOI: 10.4324/9781003510529-21

Forgiveness (see also non-judgemental)

Forgiveness is so important and rarely talked about or discussed within early childhood education and care. This is when we actively decide not to dwell on any wrongs or harbour feelings of resentment. With the children, it is about recognising they are young and not always fully in control of their emotions or actions, then keeping no record of wrongs if they do something that hurts another person or us. So if a child says, "I hate you!" in anger, in forgiving them, we will wipe the slate clean and try to restore the relationship without holding onto the negative way this probably made us feel. True forgiveness doesn't depend on whether or not someone deserves to be forgiven because it is a conscious decision we make and is linked with unconditional love. True forgiveness is difficult. It's hard to let go when we feel wronged or hurt, but when we are able to forgive someone, it releases us from these feelings of hurt, resentment, anger or bitterness.

Being able to forgive is a quality that we want to foster in our children; therefore, role modelling forgiveness is vital. Our children need to hear us use language associated with forgiveness and being sorry. However, we need to think about how we use words like "sorry" and other social conventions. Children should not be forced to say sorry to each other. In my view, it is better for children to understand the concept of (not) hurting others, feeling remorseful and being forgiven because hurting them was not our intention, rather than simply learning a word. Some children use the word sorry as if it gives them permission to act in a hurtful way or it allows them to take something, for example, take a toy from a friend, by saying sorry immediately and assuming everything is OK. They might insist, "I said sorry!" as if that means the other child should no longer feel upset. This just demonstrates a lack of understanding about what being remorseful means.

DOI: 10.4324/9781003510529-22

SAYING SORRY – A PRACTITIONER'S VIEW

When childminding, I looked after Harriet, who sometimes pinched or hurt other children when she was cross with them. She often used the word "sorry," but it didn't seem to prevent her from hurting others. On reflection with her parents, we realised that insisting that Harriet say sorry had led to her thinking it was a magic word that makes things better. We decided that at home and in my setting, we would reframe her thinking and try to enable her to explore the meaning of the word sorry. We explained to Harriet that sorry means you wish you hadn't hurt someone and you would try not to do it again. We used emotion coaching techniques, teaching Harriet that it is not OK to pinch other children when she is cross, and we also taught her alternatives to saying sorry, such as offering someone a hug or giving them a toy. I tried to role model using emotion words and saying sorry alongside alternative actions too. Over time, I noticed that Harriet hurt other children less and appeared to understand the concept of forgiveness and being sorry better.

Generosity

Generosity is when we do kind things or offer our time, talents and experiences without expecting thanks or a reward of any kind, going over and above the basics. We can be generous with the children by being kind, caring, considerate and spending time to support them. Being generous is not about doing enough; it's so much more than that. It's about going over and above expectations. An example of this is when a child lost their favourite small toy in our setting. We went out of our way to search for it and spent a lot of time looking for the toy. This is a way of being generous toward the children. Generosity is linked with kindness, and we can role model this to the children.

GENEROSITY OF TIME – A PRACTITIONER'S VIEW

Willow Children's Centre

In order to be attuned to children's interests, needs and emotions, staff get to know their children really well and are generous in the amount of time they spend with them. For example, I was supporting R's transition from toddler room to nursery by tuning into his needs and interests and spending time playing alongside him on a daily basis. Building this relationship was key to a successful transition.

 DOI: 10.4324/9781003510529-23

Gentleness

Another quality we can role model and want to foster in children is gentleness. Gentleness is being tender, kind and using soft touch. We may also think about being gentle as being kind, calm and considerate in our actions, words and interactions. We often use the term "gentle hands" in order to help children understand they need to be soft in their touch and help them to recognise their own strength. We will do this in relation to our physical interactions with each other and also in relation to using resources in our settings. When I was childminding, one of our house rules was, "We look after toys and equipment so that things are safe and clean for us and for others to play with," and when implementing this rule, I often used the term "gentle hands" which was also a phrase we used when encouraging gentle interactions with other children. As I cared for children of different ages, I often looked after a baby alongside toddlers and preschool-aged children. The toddlers needed a little help and guidance when interacting with the baby, and I role-modelled being gentle and kind continuously!

GENTLE HANDS – A PRACTITIONER'S VIEW

Willow Children's Centre

This photo was a result of interactions in the baby room around being gentle; practitioners role modelling through role play, using puppets and through stories. Also acknowledging children's feelings helps them feel comfortable and more able to understand and express what's upsetting them.

We have adopted a loving pedagogy with the children in the baby room and noticed the children using similar actions.

As adults, we use a range of strategies to support children in regulating their emotions, thoughts and behaviour, and the children have been observing, learning and making links to their own behaviour. By creating clear boundaries and behavioural expectations, we work as co-regulators to acknowledge and validate children's feelings and model appropriate language and behaviour. We try to turn incidents into opportunities that children can learn from. For example, the photo shows two children hugging after an incident. Whilst playing and exploring with magnets, making necklaces and other things, Child R turned around and snatched Child L's magnet. In response to this, Child L pushed Child R. The adult supporting the children reminded them to use "gentle hands" and reminded Child L to use her words and say, "stop, please." This prompted Child R to say "cuddle" as she approached Child L for a hug. The two children hugged and then continued with their play. The Children have further applied this loving pedagogy approach to the resources in the room. For instance, a few days ago, the children were indoors playing and exploring with the new balance scale. Due to the novelty of the scales, the children were excited and keen to have a go. However, with everyone so excited, they struggled to share. When I noticed this happen, I moved down to their level and explained that we had to look after our resources. I mentioned that we needed gentle hands with the balance scales, or they might break, and if they break, we wouldn't be able to use them. I moved closer to the scale and modelled how to play with the scales, slowly placing the objects onto the scales and waiting for the scales to move. After I finished, I said, "R's turn," and handed over an object for the child to use. The children observed as I did this. Shortly after, Child E then said out loud, "gentle hands," as she stroked her hands gently. I responded, "yes, gentle hands with the scales." For the next 20 to 30 minutes, Child E approached every child that used the scales and told them "gentle hands," encouraging everyone to be gentle with the resources.

Hold in mind

Holding children in mind is part of a loving pedagogy, and it describes when we think about children even when they are not there when we incorporate their interests and fascinations into our setting and put provisions in place for specific children. Holding children in mind is about knowing our children well, considering their needs and responding to them, even when we are not with them. Veronica Read[39] says that when practitioners hold children in mind, they, "attune to their cues so their needs are met promptly and appropriately" and children should feel "loved and delighted in, for who [they] are, rather than for what [they] might be doing."[40]

As a parent, I think about my own children or people that I love when I am not with them; for example, I might be shopping and notice a particular book and think my daughter would love that, or I might see some food on offer and know that my family would enjoy eating it – so these close relationships impact my life at all times. It was similar when I was working directly with children; I might go for a walk and notice some conkers and think, so-and-so would love these, or see an advert for a new film and remember that a child in my class was going to see it and find myself wondering if they enjoyed the movie. I used to think about the children when I was with them but also held them in mind when I was not with them. Part of a loving pedagogical approach is about holding children in mind, noticing them, meeting their needs and thinking about them regularly.

DOI: 10.4324/9781003510529-25

HOLDING CHILDREN IN MIND – A PRACTITIONER'S VIEW

Cinnamon Brow CE Primary School Nursery

Just as we, the adults within the setting, differ in our interests and personalities, so do our children. No two cohorts of children will ever be the same, and so it is by observing children and really getting to know

them that we will be able to identify what we need to do to enhance the space to meet the needs (and wants!) of the children.

When planning a particular enhancement for our continuous provision based on a child's interests, we think about how it can be incorporated throughout the whole provision, inside and outside, and not just in one area. For example, one group of children was really interested in dinosaurs, so we thought as broadly as possible. We built a dinosaur jungle with our children in a tuff tray, used large bricks to build a dinosaur cave outside, involved the children to create a gloopy swamp in our water area, sourced dinosaur books, counted dinosaurs, weighed dinosaurs, created an area with fake grass and sand for the dinosaurs to live outside, added dinosaur themed writing paper on mini clipboards and painted with dinosaurs to encourage and enhance mark-making.

When planning provocations, it is really important to make them purposeful and to understand the reasoning and rationale behind the ideas, i.e., what am I hoping my children will learn from this? Or which skills will I be developing through these enhancements? Again, knowing your children inside out is imperative – and a great way to do this is through observation! Planning our learning environments to follow the needs of our children can be both exciting and challenging. Despite its challenges, we have learnt that there is nothing more rewarding than to watch our children learn and grow in a space that holds them in mind and is truly tailored to meet their individual learning needs.

A loving pedagogy should be inclusive by nature, which means if we adopt a loving pedagogy we should try to include everyone and remove any barriers to participation. Inclusive practice seeks to be equitable and treat individuals according to their needs or circumstances rather than treating everyone the same and having a one-size-fits-all policy. I saw two great images which illustrate this; the first image shows some friends trying to go on a bike ride where everyone is given the same bike: a tall person, a medium-sized person, a wheelchair user and a child. The bike only fits the medium-sized person, so three people were excluded from the bike ride. The second image shows everyone being given a bike to suit their needs or situation: a large bike for the tall person, an average bike for the medium-sized person, an accessible three-wheeled bike for the wheelchair user and a small bike with stabilizers for the child. Now everyone can go on the bike ride. This is equity in practice.

Ways that we can be inclusive include:

- Removing any barriers to participation and learning, enabling everyone to engage fully in the life of the setting;
- Promoting a sense of belonging and keeping relationships central to our practice;
- Ensuring children can see themselves and their families represented throughout our setting in terms of staffing, policies, displays and resources;
- Focusing on the unique child and seeing children's ability and potential;
- Celebrating similarities and diversity and challenging discrimination if/when we encounter it;

- Adopting a strengths-based approach to supporting children with additional needs or disabilities;
- Auditing resources and books to ensure they are free from stereotypical images or discriminatory views;
- Adopting inclusive strategies such as using sign language, visual timetables and emotion coaching.

INCLUSIVE PRACTICE – A PRACTITIONER'S VIEW

Willow Children's Centre

Many policies in our setting, especially the Special Needs and Disability Policy, highlight the importance of inclusive practice. We aim to provide a broad, balanced, and high-quality curriculum which is accessible to and supports children with SEND, taking into account their interests, preferences and individual needs.

For example, a child who is not mobile and uses the standing frame to move around, as well as the special chair for sitting to support his core muscles, is exposed to all activities that are on offer for other children as part of the curriculum.

During free play, this child can explore indoors and the garden while being pushed on the standing frame. An adult would provide a variety of stimuli to his brain by engaging this child in sensory experiences that other children are accessing independently, such as water, sand, playdough and natural materials of different textures. These sensory experiences are presented in a personalised manner, for example, water, sand, or playdough in front of the child, either on the standing frame or at the table, which provides an opportunity to look at the resources and explore with his hands.

Even though this child has no language and his hand movements are not coordinated, an adult working with him is attuned to any gestures or sounds that the child would make, and an adult reciprocates through shared attention, words, gestures and enjoyment together. We recognise the importance of taking into account the wishes, views and feelings of children. These can be expressed in a range of ways. By being in tune with the children and close observation, practitioners can support interactions and dialogue with children by using objects as well as visual prompts and photos for a better understanding and enabling children to express what they like doing and what they find difficult. Using the Makaton alongside words also helps to communicate with some children.

Practitioners can build on their knowledge about children and better understand children's views by observing the choices they make, what they like to do and what they avoid. These views will be brought to inform discussion and decisions at each stage of planning for the next steps in development for each child. Through this inclusive practice, we ensure that the needs of all children are met.

Independence

During early childhood, children are becoming more and more independent, and we actively promote this though our policy and practice. Independence is not just about children accessing resources without needing adult help; it is also about resolving conflicts, problem solving and coping with their emotions without us. We want to teach children strategies that they can use when the adult is not with them, so in a way, we need to do ourselves out of a job!

We can teach children how to distract themselves by singing songs and rhymes or by teaching children practical responses to emotions, such as jumping when feeling excited, running in our outside area when feeling angry and cuddling a trusted adult when feeling sad, which gives them an outlet and something to do. We can also teach them grounding, relaxation and mindfulness techniques or how to use yoga and breathing exercises to help them calm.

Many providers use the zones of regulation[41] to help the children understand and identify their emotions, whilst others may use emotional response scales or mirrors and photos. The aim here is to enable children to be more emotionally literate and recognise, name and label their feelings. The more we can model different emotions and use language associated with them, the more emotionally literate our children will become.

In addition, using emotion coaching techniques and promoting problem-solving also helps children to resolve conflicts, develop self-regulation and resilience and recover from emotional outbursts or hurts and upsets.

DOI: 10.4324/9781003510529-27

RESOLVING UPSETS INDEPENDENTLY – A PRACTITIONER'S VIEW

Archway and Willow Children's Centres

Loving pedagogy is embedded in our preschool class. Staff uses a range of strategies to support children in regulating their emotions, behaviour and interactions with peers. We see conflicts as a learning opportunity. Using real-life scenarios as a teaching tool has supported the children's independent problem-solving. Children are adopting loving pedagogy strategies to manage their interactions with peers.

The example that follows demonstrates the children's ability to settle their differences emotionally, physically, and sensitively during an interaction.

A was upset and told an adult that S said they couldn't play. The adult acknowledged how A felt and asked if they had explained to S that their response had upset them. This prompted A to approach S and explain that they really wanted to play and felt sad and lonely being left out. S listened carefully and then explained that they couldn't play because they were telling everyone what to do. S said they were upset, too, because they didn't want to play that way. A thought for a moment, then said they wanted to play and would listen to everyone. S looked directly at their friend and stated, "sorry you are upset," and hugged them. Then, they continued with their play.

Joy

Joy is defined as a feeling of great happiness or pleasure in something. Working with young children can be a very joyful profession. Children are naturally joyful, will bring joy into most things they do and have the ability to find joy in the simplest things. We can learn a lot from them. My friend and colleague, Ben Kingston-Hughes, writes about joy in his new book *Why Children Need Joy: The fundamental truth about childhood*[42] and shares how joyful interactions can help children to thrive. If you ever have the chance to hear Ben speak, grasp it with both hands because it is certainly a joyful experience! He lights up the room with his stories about children he has worked with and how he sees bringing joy into their lives as a privilege and necessity!

As an early years practitioner, I notice young children when I'm out and about and can't help but notice how those around them often smile or laugh at the funny things they do and say. There is something very magical about watching a child play and noticing how they bring joy into the lives of those they meet. Therefore, joy should certainly form part of a loving pedagogy and link beautifully with playfulness, which should also feature heavily within our practice. Julie Fisher[18] suggests that effective practitioners enjoy the company of children, and I would add that we are in a privileged position where we get paid to play!

DOI: 10.4324/9781003510529-28

Kindness

A loving approach always chooses kindness. Being kind is when we are friendly, considerate and do what we can to make others happy or to promote their wellbeing. It is more than just being a nice person. It is doing something intentionally or acting in a way which will bring happiness or goodness to another person. In addition, research from the Bedari Kindness Institute[43] at the University of California found that kindness is contagious! When someone witnesses a kind act, they are more likely to be kind themselves.[44] This has implications for our work with children; the more we role model kindness and share stories about the kindness of others, the more kind everyone will become!

KINDNESS JAR – A PRACTITIONER'S VIEW

Archway Children's Centre

We have introduced the concept of the "kindness jar," which really encourages everyone to develop an understanding of being part of a team and how to interact collaboratively and develop a strong sense of self within the group.

We have a regular reflection circle where the children can share the kind deeds that they did throughout the session with all of us and then place a heart in the jar. It is a very empowering strategy and really enables them to look after their friends, work as a team and look after their environment. This is the beginning of children developing and understanding empathy.

Another thing in relation to kindness is about being kind to children. We are often in a position where we can do a kind thing or not do a kind thing. For example, a child might really, really want the green cup, and it is within our power to let them have the green cup, but many adults would not let the child have the cup because they believe the child needs to learn that they cannot always have what they want all the time. Although technically this is true, is this really the time to teach it? Do all the other children desperately want this green cup? How will the child feel about getting the cup? How would they feel if they don't get it? What are the implications for everyone, staff included? It is my view that when a child has a particular fascination with a colour, it is probably schematic and they are going through a phase where they have a strong urge that life is great when they have green things and life is not worth living when they don't! As adults, we can see the bigger picture and see it isn't a big deal for us, it's just a cup . . . but for the child, in that moment, it is a big deal. So if we can be kind and give them the cup and don't – we are deliberately being unkind!

SAYING YES AND CHOOSING KINDNESS – A CHILDMINDER'S VIEW

As adults, I think we need to say yes more! My default setting used to be to say no to a child before I'd even thought fully about what they were asking! Can I bake some cookies? (Maybe later). Can I help you do the gardening? (Maybe tomorrow). Can we paint? (Another time perhaps).

Although we were often very creative, as a childminder, it was easier to say no to a last-minute request for paints rather than get the painting things out and find all the resources needed in the moment. Perhaps we only had a certain amount of time before school pick up, or perhaps the resources were high up and I'd have needed the two-step to get them. In my mind, I had good, or at least valid, reasons for saying no. What a shame and a wasted opportunity this was at times!

I have since really worked on this, tried hard to listen to the children before making a decision and trained myself to make my default setting saying yes rather than no! That way, I can save my no's for when it really matters, and for the rest of the time, I am kind and say yes more! Even if it means it's a bit more bother for me! And the wonderful thing is, the children respond so well to this; they get a lot out of our sessions together and when I do say no, they respect it more because I rarely say this now!

Listening (see also agency, advocacy and voice of the child)

Listening with love is when we intently listen, not only to the words children say or sounds they make but when we listen to try to understand what they are communicating and ascertain their views. Genuinely consulting children is part of developing a loving pedagogy and can enable our children to feel empowered. In my book *Developing a Loving Pedagogy*,[9] I share a story about Lexie, who felt listened to as her teacher valued her drawing of the "Magic Button" and incorporated this idea into their class identity as they continued to press the button throughout the year. Lexie was empowered through listening, and all our children can feel this way if we listen with love.

The Mosaic Approach[20] outlines a methodology for practitioners to listen to and consult with young children. It attempts to view the world from the children's perspective and uses a variety of methods in order to understand what children are communicating, for example, observation, map making, photography, tours of spaces, bookmaking or informal interviews. This approach is based on the belief that children are experts in their own lives with a wealth of ideas and experiences, and adults should not only seek to understand but also value children's views.

As already mentioned, when thinking about communication, spoken language is only part of the story, and the same is true for listening, because most of the ways we listen to our children do not involve words. We listen by observing them and noticing the sounds they make, their body language and how they make eye contact or what they are looking at. We can observe any gestures they make – perhaps they can point or use sign language. Sometimes, we can listen to our children through their creations, pictures, drawings or mark-making. We can read what they write or invite our children to tell us about their writing.

DOI: 10.4324/9781003510529-30

But mostly, as all behaviour is communication, we will be listening to them through their behaviour. We can observe what they do, what their interests are, where they play and how long they play there. If a child spends a long time in a certain area or with a particular resource, we can assume they like it. We can notice who they play with, too, and mentally note their interactions. Playing alongside children is a great way to listen to their thoughts and opinions, as is asking questions to supplement our understanding.

LISTENING WITH LOVE – A PRACTITIONER'S VIEW

Conewood Children's Centre

Loving Pedagogy and trauma-informed approaches are core principles of Conewood Children's Centre's curriculum. We emphasise continual and robust interactions as essential pillars in nurturing children's learning and developmental journeys.

This case study documents Ray's experience as he moved from the toddler room to the preschool room at the age of thirty-two months. Ray had a short attention span and found receptive communication and verbal expression of his feelings and needs difficult. He frequently objected to rules in an attempt to find attachment, disrupted group activities, and occasionally acted disruptively towards his peers.

Understanding how crucial it was to build a relationship of trust with Ray, we used our professional love for him to tailor daily interactions to his specific interests and needs. At the same time, efforts were directed towards cultivating a collaborative and supportive relationship with Ray's family, characterised by active listening, empathetic understanding, and sustained patience throughout his journey.

Following a consistent four-week period of focused one-on-one engagement and reciprocal interactions, notable progress emerged in Ray's behaviour. He showed an ability to express his needs verbally and participate in small group activities, singing, dancing and playing musical instruments. In addition, he demonstrated initiative in learning new skills, such as counting objects, numeral recognition and identifying his name on the self-register.

Ray's learning journey was significantly impacted by the implementation of a loving pedagogy approach based around the practice of "listening with love" to the child and his parents. It created a safe and supportive environment that enabled him to overcome early obstacles and engage with a range of learning opportunities.

Love languages (words of affirmation, quality time, gifts, touch and acts of service)

Chapman and Campbell[6] suggest that there is a difference between being loved and feeling loved, and we all have preferred ways of feeling loved. They suggest there are five love languages: words of affirmation, quality time, gifts, touch and acts of service. If we find out our children's love languages and then speak these languages, our children will feel more loved as a result. I also suggest that this will have a knock-on impact on children's learning, as being loved adds to their sense of belonging, feelings of safety and security and provides a good foundation upon which they can learn and develop.

LOVE LANGUAGES – A PRACTITIONER'S VIEW

Willow Children's Centre

F had just transitioned from the toddler room to the nursery room. He had visited several times, and his parents had a meeting with the former key person and the new one, so strategies and interests were shared. The consistent approach around acknowledging the children's feelings and being in tune with these is implemented in all our rooms, and our "Understanding and supporting positive behaviour" policy is shared with parents. F was finding it particularly difficult transitioning from the breakfast room to the garden as he starts at 9.00, and it is a busy period, so the key person supported his transition by having warm snuggle time in the outdoor reading corner, reading some of his favourite stories. The key person was aware of what F likes and was able to find stories linked to his interests, which supported his regulation.

DOI: 10.4324/9781003510529-31

This photo is a good example of Love Languages in practice; F's key person spent quality time and used warm physical touch with him and gave him support with this transition as an act of service and the gift of tuning into his interests and using them to support him to regulate; offered words of affirmation through acknowledgement and expression of his feelings.

We might notice a child's love language is **words of affirmation** because they will use words to show their love to us. They might compliment us on our clothing or hair or tell us they love us. We can then use words in return to demonstrate our love.

Quality time is about how we show our love by spending time with the people we love. One of our children might sometimes be nicknamed our shadow and want to always be with us. So we can save them a place next to us, respond to their attention-seeking behaviour by seeing it as attachment-seeking,[45] and endeavour to spend quality time with them.

We might observe a child giving us or another member of staff a pebble or flower in the outside area. This is a love token, and it's highly likely that their love language is **gifts.** We can demonstrate our love to the child by reciprocating this, giving them a stone or conker we have found and putting the gifts they present us with on display.

Touch is a little more obvious to notice, as children will want to hold our hand, cuddle us and use physical touch to demonstrate their love to us. Again, we can use consented touch back. Praise them with a high-five, offer them a hug goodbye and squeeze their shoulder as we walk past.

Acts of service is about when children might want to help us or we do things for them. Some children do things for each other, too; they have a natural sense of servitude. Perhaps they are destined to work in the hospitality industry! These actions could demonstrate a love language of acts of service and overlap with being kind to one another.

HELPING OUR FRIENDS – A PRACTITIONER'S VIEW

As a setting, we encourage kindness and celebrate kind actions when we see them. We often notice children helping each other and doing things for their friends. The following photograph shows one child helping another to put on their wellie boots.

Nurture

In our book *Love and Nurture in the Early Years,*[46] Aaron Bradbury and I explain nurture in the following way:

> To nurture someone is to care deeply for them and help them to grow and thrive. In this sense our early childhood provision is predominantly about nurturing children. This goes hand in hand with loving children. It would be impossible to truly love a child without nurturing them, because real love is active and wants the very best for the other person.

We go on to share the interconnectedness of love and nurture:[47]

> When we consider ideas of love and nurture within an early childhood context, they appear to be inseparable from each other. Where does loving stop and nurturing begin, and vice versa? Often the phrase lovingly nurtured is used when thinking about tending to a garden which implies a longer-term commitment. To lovingly nurture our children we meet their immediate needs with a long-term view, just as we might nurture a seed, knowing that we are helping a plant or flower to grow. Our focus is broadly on the bigger picture, however, we still need to manage the detail as we feed and water the seedling and make sure the environment offers enough light and nutrients daily for it to grow.

Nurture is a word that is often used in conjunction with our loving ethos. It describes our intentional practices which aim to support our children and help them to grow and develop. For example, we may nurture our children through the way we interact with them, our use of our voice, how our key person approach promotes secure relationships and through providing an accessible, stimulating and enabling learning environment. Our loving pedagogy nurtures our children.

DOI: 10.4324/9781003510529-32

Patience

In my book *Developing a Loving Pedagogy*,[9] I talk about the passage from the Bible which states, "Love is patient . . ." and I believe practising patience to be an important aspect of a loving approach. Being patient with children empowers them as we take time to listen and respond sensitively to them. It tells children that we value them and accept them as they are and demonstrates our love in a very practical way. Being patient is not easy, but it is a skill we can practise, develop and eventually master!

When we exhibit patience, we have the capacity to put up with being delayed or suffering in a small way without becoming anxious or annoyed. Being patient with the children means we remain calm and can wait for our children to complete things in their own time or accept that we may need to repeat an instruction several times before it is carried out. In order to be patient, we have to remain focused on the child and their needs and put our own needs and feelings aside, at least in that moment. So, for example, if a child desperately wants to put their own shoes on, but we know it will take a lot longer than if we help them, we should listen to the child. We may want to get out of the door faster, but at that moment, we may need to wait patiently until they are ready. In the long run, encouraging independence will allow the child to develop their skills and make getting out of the house faster once they can do things for themselves.

We can learn to be more patient by working out what triggers us or if there are any times when we are less patient, then we can plan for these situations. If you need to, allow extra time for transitions, and if, like me, you get "hangry" (angry when hungry), take a snack with you! Notice any signs or signals in your body which indicate you are losing your temper or becoming impatient, then try to take a moment to recover, practice breathing techniques or allow yourself a break. If you

DOI: 10.4324/9781003510529-33

have lost patience with a child, apologise and explain the reasons why. This role models taking responsibility for our actions and being kind and caring. Lastly, remember that in being patient with our children, we are expressing our love, accepting their short-term dependence and having more developmentally appropriate expectations.

THE IMPORTANCE OF BEING PATIENT – A PRACTITIONER'S VIEW

Mountford Manor

Pedro has just turned four and attends nursery five mornings a week. He has a language delay and only speaks using single words; however, he has a wide vocabulary and a wonderful imagination. During conversations, adults playing with Pedro need to remain patient and allow him time to respond and say what he wants to say. He can become frustrated when he cannot get his thoughts across quickly enough and can struggle in play with his peers due to his language delay.

Pedro enjoys small world play and wanted to share a story with me, his teacher.

He holds up a toy dragon:

Pedro – "Dragon."
Teacher – "You have a blue dragon."
Pedro – "Man."
Teacher – "The man is on the dragon."
Pedro – "Flying."
Teacher – "The man is flying on the dragon."
Pedro – "Yeah. Argh, falling."
Teacher – "The man has fallen off the dragon."
Pedro – "Save."
Teacher – "The dragon is going to save the man."
Pedro – "Loop loop."
Teacher – "The dragon is doing loop the loops."

Pedro – "Gotcha."

Teacher – "The man was flying on the dragon's back and fell off. The dragon did loop the loops, and he saved the man."

Pedro – "Yeah, happy."

Teacher – "The man and the dragon are happy now."

Pedro gave a big smile that his story had been heard, understood and retold back to him.

Professional Love

The term "Professional Love" was coined by Dr Jools Page as a result of her research project *Professional Love in Early Years Settings* (PLEYS).[48] In 2021, Dr Page[49] was awarded the *Association of Infant Mental Health UK Louise Emmanuel Award* for her characterisation of "Professional Love" – this prestigious award recognises her significant contribution, in terms of practice, research and policy, to infant mental health. Dr Page has written many research papers, articles and chapters for books about her approach, and it was her 2011 work, *Do mothers want professional carers to love their babies?*,[2] alongside reading about love languages,[6] that initially inspired my work in this area.

The term "Professional Love" describes when adults use love, care and intimacy within childcare practices and frame it within a professional context. Page identifies that some practitioners are able to "de-centre" and remove their needs from the equation, for example, remaining focused on the child and responding to their needs at all times.[48] She believes that this helps them not to become too attached to the children. I built on Dr Page's ideas around professional love when I discussed a loving pedagogy which describes a whole pedagogical approach incorporating professional love.

DOI: 10.4324/9781003510529-34

Relationships are at the heart of effective practice, and children are social beings from birth and developing social competence as they grow. We can build strong attachments and relationships with our children, getting to know them really well and role-modelling how to be a good friend; for example, friends help each other, and friends are kind and gentle. Although we will teach children to be *friendly* to everyone, I believe they do not have to be *friends* with everyone and we should not insist they play with everyone. This links with consent, as children have the right to choose who they play with, and making them play with others would go against the principles of consent.

FRIENDSHIP – A PRACTITIONER'S VIEW

Archway and Willow Children's Centres

We encourage children to build friendships with each other and role model this. We have found that we observe our children being kind and caring to each other. For example, helping to put each other's shoes on or helping to do up a zip for their friend.

DOI: 10.4324/9781003510529-35

Respect

When we respect someone, we treat them in a way that considers their feelings, wishes and upholds their rights. Being respectful is a loving response and feeling respected helps someone have self-worth and feel valued. We need to role model having respect for others and always speak in respectful ways to other people. Talking down to someone, holding them in contempt or believing someone isn't as good as you are all disrespectful ways of behaving and thinking. We need to be counter to this and demonstrate respect through our words and actions, for example, through kind and loving actions, looking after resources and equipment and celebrating differences and diversity.

The University of West London[50] offers these 10 ideas of how to show respect to one another:

1. Be kind and courteous;
2. Be polite, avoid interrupting or causing disturbances;
3. Listen to others and respect differences in beliefs and opinions;
4. Think before you speak, your language and tone;
5. Lend a helping hand or ear and practice compassion;
6. Avoid gossip and any conversations that may be considered discriminatory or bullying;
7. Respect personal space and personal property;
8. Understand everyone has their own experiences and beliefs;
9. Speak up if others around you are being disrespectful;
10. Be willing to evolve and admit mistakes.

DOI: 10.4324/9781003510529-36

BEING CONSIDERATE TO OTHERS – A PRACTITIONER'S VIEW

Archway Children's Centre

Nursery life provides endless opportunities for our children to develop extremely important life skills. It is both an inclusive and diverse environment where the children learn how to respect their peers irrespective of their differences and treat one another in a kind and considerate manner. This is a daily, fluid narrative that takes place throughout our sessions. The children are encouraged to use their gentle hands and words and help each other whilst sharing both the environment and resources. We regularly see children helping each other and being considerate in their interactions.

Adults give children the opportunity and the tools to self-regulate and understand how to navigate big feelings in a harmonious manner and learn how to be respectful to others through positive role modelling, stories revolving around feelings and the use of Persona dolls. We also empower our children by acting out first-hand experiences that the children are facing, such as issues around sharing and using their voices to express their thoughts in a clear but kind way.

Being responsive to the children's needs and tapping into their interests and fascinations is another way of showing children we value them. Julie Fisher[18] talks about interacting sensitively with children in our everyday practice. This is about being attuned to children and noticing their needs, wants and wishes, then acting upon this information and interacting, bearing this in mind. Sometimes, our response is actually to wait, listen, notice and observe rather than actually do anything. At other times, our response may be to intervene or act. We can also ensure that we are proactive rather than reactive when supporting their behaviour; this is the best response to adopt because it is preventative and aims to stop challenging behaviours before they arise.

BEING RESPONSIVE TO THE CHILDREN'S NEEDS – A PRACTITIONER'S VIEW

Archway Children's Centre

R and Z met in the toddler room at Archway Children's Centre. R has been finding it challenging to regulate his feelings and needs support in recognising them and expressing them. His outbursts have led to conflicts with other children in the room. Z needed some support with social interactions. They both have a shared interest in superheroes and vehicles and often play together, pretending to be their favourite characters.

During a group activity, the teacher encouraged the children to work together to build a house using wooden blocks. R and Z were excited to participate and happily worked together to create

DOI: 10.4324/9781003510529-37

an imaginative house. R was particularly interested in building the bedroom, while Z enjoyed creating the kitchen. As they worked on the project together, they started to show signs of positive social and emotional development. Their shared interest in building a tall house helped them bond and collaborate effectively, developing important social skills such as cooperation, communication, and problem-solving. They also learned to express their emotions through play, which helps them develop emotional intelligence.

A few days later, R and Z started to run around the garden, pretending to fly an airplane and be passengers on the plane. R even carried a box, pretending that it was a suitcase. Their pretend play in the garden further strengthened their bond and enriched their play experience. They continued to communicate and cooperate with each other, taking turns carrying the suitcase and navigating through the imaginary skies. This activity also encouraged imaginative thinking, creativity, and problem-solving, as they had to come up with new scenarios and overcome obstacles in their pretend journey.

During a different activity, R and Z both brought their favourite cars to play with. R had two cars, one red and one yellow, while Z had one blue car. As they were playing, Z expressed interest in playing with one of R's cars. Initially, R hesitated to share his toys, but with some encouragement from the teacher, he eventually shared. This act of sharing was a positive example of R's social and emotional development. By sharing his toy, R showed empathy towards Z and demonstrated an understanding of the importance of sharing and cooperation in social situations. In addition, this act of sharing helped to strengthen their bond and further develop their positive relationship, as Z was grateful for the opportunity to play with R's car. The teacher praised R for his willingness to share and encouraged him to continue to show kindness and empathy towards his peers. This experience helped R understand the value of sharing and the positive impact it can have on his relationships with others. It also helped Z feel included and appreciated, which contributed to his own social and emotional development.

These examples show that attuning and being responsive to the children's interests and needs can have a significant impact on children's social and emotional development, just as it did for R and Z. Activities based on shared interests can have a positive impact on children, especially in terms of their social and emotional development. R and Z's shared interest in superheroes and vehicles helped them bond and collaborate effectively, developing important social skills such as cooperation, communication, problem-solving, imaginative thinking and creativity.

Safe and secure

Children have a right to feel safe and secure in all aspects of their lives. I believe that when children are loved, it contributes to their feelings of safety and security. Many practitioners will have come across Maslow's hierarchy of needs,[7] which suggests that we need our basic needs met before we can meet our potential in life. He would argue that alongside things like food, water and shelter, our basic needs include safety and security as well as love and belonging. Sadly there are many things that get in the way of children feeling safe and secure, for example, Adverse Childhood Experiences, trauma, abuse, changes in the home or setting, starting school or nursery.

In my book, *Supporting Behaviour and Emotions*[51] I talk about the importance of feeling safe and secure:

> If I were to go on a bus journey and felt the driver was driving erratically and dangerously, I would want to get off the bus as soon as possible. Feeling unsafe is not a good way to feel. If I were to snuggle up on our sofa at home with a blanket over me and watch my favourite film I would feel really safe and secure. For me, home is a safe haven and secure base where I can relax and just be, and having time at home enables me to face the big wide world! It is vital that children feel safe and secure in their homes, but also in our settings – if they do not, they will not be ready to learn.

We can help children to feel safe and secure by:

- Adopting a loving pedagogy and ensuring our children feel loved, respected and valued;
- Building secure attachments and prioritising relationships, using our key person approach effectively;

DOI: 10.4324/9781003510529-38

- Welcoming children and families and promoting a sense of belonging in our setting;
- Getting to know the children well, incorporating their interests into our provision;
- Working closely with families and responding sensitively to any changes;
- Being flexible enough to support children's changing needs whilst providing a predictable routine with realistic expectations and boundaries;
- Supporting children through change and transition;
- Promoting children's rights and being advocates for them;
- Whenever possible, offering children choices or input into decisions, empowering them and helping them to feel informed about things happening in their lives;
- Ensuring children's basic needs have been met.

Safeguarding

Interestingly, the first act of parliament in relation to the protection of children was the "Prevention of Cruelty to, and Protection of, Children Act" of 1889,[52] during the reign of Queen Victoria. Commonly known as the Children's Charter, this was an important first step preventing cruelty to children and paved the way for our safeguarding and child protection legislation of today. We now view safeguarding as our highest priority within early childhood settings, and it is an important consideration in relation to a loving pedagogy.

We must ensure that children are protected and that our practices safeguard them; however, we must also ensure that any fears we may have about child protection do not inhibit our practice,[53] for example, in relation to using positive touch with our children. Sometimes, I encounter a setting with a "no touch" policy or similar, which has erred rather too much on the side of caution. These policies usually prevent a child from cuddling a practitioner, or a practitioner from using touch to praise a child with, for example, a high-five or a squeeze on the shoulder. Although I can understand where these policies stem from, research tells us about the vital importance of touch,[54] and I personally see such policies as neglectful and damaging to children.

In England, the safeguarding statutory guidance *Working Together to Safeguard Children*[55] states, "Anyone working with children should see and speak to the child, listen to what they say, observe their behaviour, take their views seriously, and work with them and their families and the people who know them well when deciding how to support their needs." This nests beautifully within a loving pedagogical approach which seeks to put the child at the centre of their practice. With a policy in place which outlines how we will use touch as part of a loving pedagogy, we can stand firm that our approach not only safeguards children but also enables them to feel loved.

DOI: 10.4324/9781003510529-39

Self-compassion

Self-compassion is about feeling compassionate for oneself, so noticing you are suffering and then feeling moved and responding to that pain. So, I acknowledge when I am going through a difficult time or am feeling hurt and then am patient with myself, just as I would be patient with someone else if they were going through this. Dr Kristin Neff[56] suggests we ask ourselves, "How can I comfort and care for myself in this moment?" and instead of criticising ourselves for being inadequate or not being perfect, we replace this narrative with kind and understanding thoughts.

Children need to learn self-compassion so that they can treat themselves kindly even if things do not go the way they want them to. We need to role-model this too, perhaps saying something like, "Oh dear, I didn't manage to finish my jobs for today; I tried really hard but still ran out of time. That's OK. I can start on them again tomorrow." Or "Uh oh! I've coloured this red when I meant to colour it blue. Never mind, we all make mistakes and it looks nice red." There is a good book called *Beautiful Oops* by Barney Saltzberg[57] which shows how mistakes can be turned into something positive. Another game we can play is making splodges of paint or scribbling on paper and then turning it into a picture, again role modelling how order can come out of chaos!

DOI: 10.4324/9781003510529-40

If you have high self-esteem, you feel good about yourself, like yourself and see yourself as competent and capable. Often, this is a result of your external experiences and the way you perceive other people to view you. Having a good level of self-esteem contributes to our feelings of self-worth, which concerns your belief in your own value as a person and your ability to see yourself as worth something. Our self-esteem can fluctuate depending on our experiences and the way others validate us or appear to value our achievements, whereas self-worth is less superficial and not as dependent on others. They often go hand in hand, and we want to encourage feelings of both self-esteem and self-worth in our children.

Having high levels of self-esteem helps children to feel confident, be more resilient, face challenges and overcome difficulties. In order to have this high level of self-esteem, you need to feel valued and worthwhile (self-worth), which is where adopting a loving pedagogy fits in. The loving relationships we develop with our children will hugely impact their feelings of self-esteem and self-worth.

SELF-WORTH – A PRACTITIONER'S VIEW

Archway and Willow Children's Centres

This is a lovely example of how a child confidently enjoys his own space and self. In our setting, we have a mirror which is deliberately placed at child height.

In the following series of photographs, you can see how J first talks to his reflection, then sings and finally dances along with

DOI: 10.4324/9781003510529-41

his reflection. It was a wonderful moment to witness, and shows how he is developing feelings of self-worth and confidence in himself as a singer, dancer and great mover!

Self-regulation (see also co-regulation)

Self-regulation is difficult to define, and Shanker, Hopkins and Davidson[58] found 400 different definitions in the psychological literature alone! When we are self-regulated, we can manage our thoughts and feelings and we are resilient enough to cope with life and everything it throws at us. When we have self-regulation, we are also able to maintain focus and attention and inhibit our impulses. In addition, when we are self-regulated, we feel a positive sense of wellbeing and are ready to learn. The opposite of having self-regulation is feeling dysregulated. This is when someone feels out of sorts, emotionally unstable and not OK. They usually have a low sense of wellbeing and, in this state, they are not able to think clearly and are not ready to learn.

In our book *Nurturing Self-Regulation in Early Childhood*,[59] my colleague Wendy and I define self-regulation as,

> the capacity of a person to both cognitively and emotionally cope with the ups and downs of daily life as well as the dispositions and skills needed to do this. It includes being in control of our emotions, adjusting our behaviour, planning our actions, empathising with others and developing social confidence, all of which promote good wellbeing.

The best way to grow self-regulation is through being in a relationship with others and through co-regulation when an adult scaffolds, role-models and supports us emotionally.

Research[60,61,62] informs us that children with high levels of self-regulation achieve more in school and have better life chances than

DOI: 10.4324/9781003510529-42

those who have not developed this skill. Self-regulation develops over a long period of time. Initially, newborn babies rely on adults to regulate their emotional states, but by 3-months-old, a baby can be distracted when upset and by 4-months-old, a baby can self-soothe. These are the beginnings of self-regulation. Usually, by the time a child is one year old, they can distract themselves and maintain joint attention with another person, usually a main carer, and by the time they are two, they will be beginning to use language alongside actions to label emotions and express their needs and wants. The development of self-regulation is closely linked to their social development, and by the age of three, children are more socially aware and will usually begin to play more cooperatively with others.[63] In addition, children develop Theory of Mind between the ages of three and six years, which is the ability of a child to recognise that other people have thoughts and feelings that could differ from theirs. This helps them to take the perspective of others, which is linked with our capability to empathise.

Here are some suggestions of how we can help to develop children's self-regulation:

- Build secure relationships with children so that they know they can trust you.
- Offer children reassurance, love and build their self-esteem.
- Remain calm and self-regulated yourself so you are available to co-regulate with children.
- Have clear behavioural expectations which are developmentally appropriate.
- Offer calm spaces and areas for children to recharge and rest.
- Ensure the environment is emotionally safe so that children can use it as a secure base and feel free to take risks and make mistakes.
- Develop an emotionally literate environment by using photos, books, resources, signs and gestures, all of which help to promote their understanding of feelings and emotions.
- Support children to understand the routine by using now/next boards, visual timetables, objects of reference and clear explanations.
- Role-model feelings and share calming strategies.

SELF-REGULATION – A PRACTITIONER'S VIEW

Archway and Willow Children's Centres

This interaction between a preschool child from the older cohort towards one of our youngest preschool pupils is another example of how loving pedagogy is embedded in our setting and how effective role-modelling with the children has enabled them to use self-regulation strategies independently.

K has learnt to self-regulate. It has been a long journey and involved a lot of support and strategies from staff. Some of the tools K uses are taking a deep breath, seeking out an adult and explaining why he is upset. K is now rarely dysregulated. When he is upset, he can self-regulate and move on quickly. In this example, K was seen using his strategies to support his younger peer. He was calm, warm, and physically supportive.

S was crying as a child had taken away an object that she had been playing with. K came over, knelt so that he could look S in the eyes, gently wiped a tear away and said, "Take a deep breath." S was pointing at the child who had taken the toy, and K explained, "It's ok, I'll get the sand timer; you can have it again soon." He then went off to get the sand timer. An adult then stepped in to acknowledge S's feelings and reassure her that they could take turns with the toy. K returned with the sand timer and turned it over, stating, "There." S had now stopped crying and began watching the sand. K had comforted his peer and found a solution.

Touch (see also consent)

For the majority of children, sensitive and positive touch is an important part of a loving relationship; however, it is important to note that some children may not like touch or want to be touched, and we must respect this. Several hormones are associated with loving and nurturing touch; sometimes, these are referred to as DOSE, dopamine, oxytocin, serotonin and endorphins. Dopamine is our brain's reward system, and oxytocin is often described as the love hormone because it is associated with childbirth and being lovingly touched. Oxytocin helps to reduce cortisol, the stress hormone. Serotonin is our mood stabiliser, which contributes to our wellbeing and happiness, and endorphins are our natural painkillers, which help to relieve stress and block pain.

We can use touch in a variety of ways and for a number of different reasons in our settings. For example, we can praise a child with a high-five, gently squeeze a child's shoulder as we walk past them and catch their eye, rub their back if they are feeling upset, hold their hand to keep them safe or allow them to sit on our lap or cuddle up for a story. There is a wealth of research[54] which highlights how vital touch is for our wellbeing and in helping us to feel loved. I advise settings to include their thoughts about touch in safeguarding policies or in their relationships or loving pedagogy policy. Part 2 thinks about this in more detail.

Unconditional love

When we love unconditionally, we love regardless of the child's behaviour or attitude. There is nothing a child can do or say that will make us love them more or less. Our love is not earned or based upon anything other than who the child is. Unconditional love says we love you, warts and all! We demonstrate unconditional love when we value and accept children, meet them where they are and hold them with positive regard. Unconditional love wants the very best and greatest good for the children in our care. We may say that we unconditionally love our children, but do they always *feel* loved? This is where we can consider identifying and speaking children's love languages.

DOI: 10.4324/9781003510529-44

Voice of the child (see also advocacy, agency and listening)

Article 12 of the United Nations Convention on the Rights of the Child[10] states,

> Parties shall assure to the child who is capable of forming his or her own views the right to express those views freely in all matters affecting the child, the views of the child being given due weight in accordance with the age and maturity of the child.

This means that children have a right to have a say in things that impact them and, whenever possible, we need to seek children's views about their lives. This is not always easy to put into practice; however, a loving pedagogy seeks to hear the voice of the child.

We can ascertain the voice of the child by:

- Directly asking them their views about a situation or issue. We need to carefully word this depending on their age and stage of development;
- Listening to any words spoken or noticing the sounds they make and listening while they play or talk with their peers;
- Noticing their body language and eye contact/eye movement;
- Noting any gestures or sign language used;
- Observing them (what they do, what their interests are, where they play, who they play with, how long they are there);
- Engaging in role play alongside children;
- Looking at their creations, drawings, pictures or mark-making;
- Reading what they write or inviting children to read it to you;
- Noticing their behaviour because all behaviour is communication;
- Using a mosaic approach[20] to listen to the child (see listening).

Warmth

Warmth is a term we often use when we think about relationships and our loving interactions. A warm relationship gives me the mental image of a hug – being close to someone and feeling affection from that person. Warmth as a practitioner is about being friendly, trustworthy, kind and loving towards the children. I read an interesting article[64] which differentiated between being warm-hearted and having a warm personality. It suggested that being warm-hearted was about being compassionate and caring, whereas having a warm personality is about how you come across to other people, for example, do you appear agreeable, empathetic, kind, generous, sociable and friendly? As early childhood practitioners, we need to be both warm-hearted and have a warm personality so that children see us as approachable, friendly, loving and kind.

In his famous (and sadly rather cruel) experiments with macaque monkeys, Harry Harlow[65] demonstrated that physical and psychological warmth is essential and valued more highly than just meeting our basic needs, as the monkeys preferred to stay close to a warm and soft cloth surrogate mother rather than a cold wire mother who provided them with food. Research[66] tells us that people perceived as being warm in terms of their personality or traits are viewed much more positively in relation to behaviour and emotions.

Interestingly, I read some research by Williams and Bargh[67] which shares that there is a link between the physical temperature of feeling warm and the interpersonal warmth of someone's personality because both evoke memories and/or feelings associated with feeling safe, secure, warm and comforted. They reiterate in their research the importance of physical warmth from caregivers in early childhood and link this with Bowlby's attachment research.[12]

DOI: 10.4324/9781003510529-46

Wellbeing

We usually use the term wellbeing to describe feeling positive, that is, feeling good about ourselves, content with life, safe and secure and having a high sense of self-esteem and self-worth. In her book *Promoting Young Children's Emotional Health and Wellbeing*,[68] my colleague and friend Sonia Mainstone-Cotton states,

> I believe one of the most important roles we have as adults is to help children to have good wellbeing, and the start of that is helping children to know that they are loved, they are special and they are unique individuals.

In addition to this, in her new book *Wellbeing Explained*[69] which is part of this book series, Sonia suggests wellbeing can be defined as when someone feels loved, safe, feels like they belong, loves themselves, feels good about who they are and are able to cope with life's difficulties. She also reiterates the importance of self-love and self-care in terms of wellbeing, too.

I would also argue that feeling loved and having a positive sense of wellbeing are inextricably linked, and wellbeing stems from being in secure relationships with others. As Read[70] confirms, "We now know due to advances and research on brain development that the key building blocks for emotional wellbeing, good mental health and future success in life are developed through close, loving and intimate relationships."

Prioritising wellbeing for both children and adults is an important part of adopting a loving pedagogy. As the saying goes, "We cannot pour from an empty cup," and we need to ensure we have a positive sense of wellbeing, too. A loving pedagogy also involves loving ourselves because this will enable us to better care for the children. When adults focus on promoting children's wellbeing the knock-on effect is that their own wellbeing tends to rise, too.

It can also be helpful to measure wellbeing in our schools and settings, using measures such as the Leuven Scales for wellbeing and involvement[71] because, as The Children's Society[72] highlights, "If schools do not measure the wellbeing of their children, but do measure their intellectual development, the latter will always take precedence." Generally speaking, people value what they measure, and if they are only measuring a child's phonics ability or whether or not they can write their name or count to 10, it may appear that these things are more important than a child's wellbeing.

SUPPORTING WELLBEING – A PRACTITIONER'S VIEW

Willow Children's Centre

In addition to a discussion around kind and caring hands, we have been talking with the children about physical wellbeing and hygiene. Adults role model respectful and consenting interactions and try to encourage independence in self-care activities, for example, asking if we can wipe a child's nose or encouraging them to do it themselves. On one occasion, a child needed a tissue and another child went to help them by getting a tissue from the box and taking it over to his friend and gently wiping her nose.

Conclusion of Part 1

I hope this first section has been useful to give you a brief overview of many of the key terms used in the context of a loving pedagogy. In the next part, you will find a list of further ideas, suggestions of places to look and websites linked with each of the definitions. I have sometimes included references to children's books, if appropriate.

DOI: 10.4324/9781003510529-48

On the following pages are some ideas for further reading or resources. Some are academic references for books I have found useful on the topic, which are self-explanatory; other ideas are links to videos or blogs and I have briefly explained what these are about. For some themes, I have also included books or resources aimed at children and have given a very brief idea of what the story covers.

Acknowledging feelings and emotions

Emotion Coaching UK Website: https://www.emotioncoachinguk.com/

Sesame Steet Resources Covering a Range of Topics, Including Children's Emotional Development: https://www.sesamestreet.org/parents/learning-areas/emotional-development

For children

Encouraging discussion about feelings: Llenas, A. (2016) *The Colour Monster*. London: Templar Publishing.

Simple story about sharing different feelings: Parr, T. (2009) *The Feelings Book*. London: Little Brown Young Readers.

Tom Percival has written lots of books which explore feelings and emotions aimed at children aged about 2–3 years and upwards.

DOI: 10.4324/9781003510529-49

Acceptance

Lansford, J. (2021) *Making Children Feel Loved and Accepted – Article Aimed at Parents but Useful for Educators.* https://www.psychologytoday.com/gb/blog/parenting-and-culture/202102/making-children-feel-loved-and-accepted

For children

Celebrating acceptance of being different: Andreae, G. (2012) *Giraffes Can't Dance.* New York: Orchard Books.
Lovely illustrated book celebrating difference: Potter, M. (2023) *The Same but Different.* London: Bloomsbury Education.

Advocacy

Barnardo's Advocacy: https://www.barnardos.org.uk/get-support/support-for-parents-and-carers/childrens-rights-advocacy
United Nations Convention on the Rights of the Child: www.unicef.org.uk/Documents/Publication-pdfs/UNCRC_PRESS200910web.pdf

For children

Beautifully illustrated version of children's rights: Castle, C. (2001) *For Every Child: The UN Convention on the Rights of the Child.* London: Red Fox.

Agency

Supporting Agency: Involving Children in Decision Making leaflet from the Australian Children's Education and Care Quality Authority. https://www.acecqa.gov.au/sites/default/files/2018-04/QA1_SupportingAgencyInvolvingChildreninDecisionMaking.pdf

For children

Celebrating and empowering children to be themselves: Henn, S. (2019) *Super Duper You*. London: Puffin.

Attachment

Bergin, C. and Bergin, D. (2009) Attachment in the classroom. *Educational Psychology Review*, 21, 141–170.

Bowlby, J. (1953) *Childcare and the Growth of Love*. London: Penguin Books.

Brooks, R. (2020) *The Trauma and Attachment Aware Classroom*. London: Jessica Kingsley.

Gerhardt, S. (2015) *Why Love Matters: How Affection Shapes a Baby's Brain*. 2nd edn. Hove: Routledge.

Music, G. (2017) *Nurturing Natures: Attachment and Children's Emotional, Sociocultural and Brain Development*. Abingdon: Routledge.

Read, V. (2014) *Developing Attachment in Early Years Settings: Nurturing Secure Relationships from Birth to Five Years*. 2nd edn. Abingdon: Routledge.

For children

Explaining attachment as if it were an invisible string connecting us to the people we love: Karst, P. (2001) *The Invisible String*. Camarillo: Devorss Publishers.

Supporting children with bereavement: Dougherty, J. (2023) *The Hare-Shaped Hole*. London: Frances Lincoln Children's Books.

Attunement

Article about *The Power of Attunement*, although written in relation to autism, this article is an interesting read and would be relevant for all children. It is available at https://cdikids.org/autism/power-attunement/

Interesting article about attunement and play: https://www.nifplay.org/what-is-play/types-of-play/attunement-play/

Belonging and welcoming

A Sense of Belonging: EYFS Card from EYFS (2008) https://www.earlyyearsmatters.co.uk/wp-content/uploads/2012/04/A-Sense-of-Belonging.pdf

For children

Exploring belonging: Davies, B. and Martin, F. (2023) *No Matter What . . . We All Belong*. London: Little Tiger Press Ltd.

Behaviour

Dix, P. (2017) *When the Adults Change, Everything Changes: Seismic Shifts in School Behaviour*. Carmarthen: Independent Thinking Press.

Extract from Tamsin's Training for Parents and Carers About Behaviour: https://www.youtube.com/watch?v=8Q7MdOucZsl

Grimmer, T. (2022) *Supporting Behaviour and Emotions in the Early Years: Strategies and Ideas for Early Years Educators*. Abingdon: Routledge.

Henderson, N. and Smith, H. (2022) *Relationship-Based Pedagogy in Primary Schools: Learning with Love*. Abingdon: Routledge.

For children

Exploring getting angry and emotional outbursts: Percival, T. (2019) *Ravi's Roar*. London: Bloomsbury Children's Books.

Thinking about how our behaviour affects others: McCloud, C. (2013) *Have You Filled a Bucket Today?* New York: Nelson Publishing.

Caring

Birth to 5 Matters Section on Care: https://birthto5matters.org.uk/care/

Noddings, N. (2002) *Starting at Home: Caring and Social Policy*. London: University of California Press.

For children

Exploring kindness through a classroom incident: Miller, P. (2020) *Be Kind*. London: Pan Macmillan.

Communication (including non-verbal)

Blank, J. and Bevan, A. (2017) *Communication and Language: An Active Approach to Developing Communication Skills*. Salisbury: Practical Preschool Books.

DfE Materials About Communication and Language in the EYFS: https://help-for-early-years-providers.education.gov.uk/communication-and-language

Sheffield Children's NHS Social Stories: https://library.sheffieldchildrens.nhs.uk/social-stories/

Compassion and sympathy

Delahooke, M. (2020) *Beyond Behaviours Using Brain Science and Compassion to Understand and Solve Children's Behavioural Challenges*. London: John Murray Press.

Video About Growing Compassion: https://www.youtube.com/watch?v=hfFV9exDmEY

For children

Aimed more at children over 4, this book explores bullying and compassion: Davies, N. (2021) *The New Girl*. Llanelli: Graffeg Limited.

Consent

NSPCC PANTS Underwear Rule: https://www.nspcc.org.uk/keeping-children-safe/support-for-parents/pants-underwear-rule/

Safe Secure Kids Teaching Children About Consent: https://www.
safesecurekids.org/themes/custom/safe_secure_kids/files/SSK-
Handout.pdf

For children

This rhyming book explores consent at children's level: Barkla, C. and
Lee, J. (2022) *From My Head to My Toes, I Say What Goes.* Victoria,
Australia: Bright Light.

Co-construction

Using the Observe-Plan-Cycle to Co-Construct the Curriculum with
Children: https://birthto5matters.org.uk/wp-content/uploads/2021/03/
PDF-22-OAP-and-co-constructing-the-curriculum.pdf
Videos explaining co-construction: https://youtube.com/playlist?list=PL
uwr7fChk2D6naGnahEKf6rYbQ6Lg72Wp&si=0O5ua3uA-UxlF45c

Co-regulation

Blog about co-regulation written by an Occupational Therapist: https://
www.theottoolbox.com/co-regulation/
Grimmer, T. and Geens, W. (2022) *Nurturing Self-regulation in Early
Childhood.* Abingdon: Routledge.
Video about self-regulation and co-regulation: https://www.youtube.
com/watch?v=RRMBHQ-Bmk0

FURTHER READING AND RESOURCES

Duty of care

Article written by secondary headteacher about professional love: Wood, A. (2013) Is professional 'love' appropriate? *SecEd Blog*, 12 September. https://www.sec-ed.co.uk/content/blogs/is-professional-love-appropriate

What 'In Loco Parentis' Means in Relation to Duty of Care, UK: https://www.lawandparents.co.uk/what-in-loco-parentis-means-you.html

Emotion coaching

Emotion Coaching UK: https://www.emotioncoachinguk.com/

Gilbert, L., Gus, L. and Rose, J. (2021) *Emotion Coaching with Children and Young People in Schools*. London: Jessica Kingsley.

For children

Campbell Books (2022) *Little Big Feelings Collection 6 Books Set (I Like to be Kind, Sometimes I am Worried, When I am Happy, Sometimes I am Angry, I Can Say Sorry, I Can Be Patient)*. London: Campbell Books. Janet Rose (Emotion Coaching UK and Norland College) shares her expertise for parents/adults in each of these books.

Empathy

Dr Brené Brown video: https://www.youtube.com/watch?v=1Evwgu369Jw&vl=en-GB

What Is Empathy Article: https://greatergood.berkeley.edu/topic/empathy/definition

105

For children

Exploring how it feels when things go wrong and how listening to others can help: Doerrfeld, C. (2020) *The Rabbit Listened*. London: Scallywag Press.

Highlighting the importance of connecting with other people: Zephaniah, B. (2023) *People Need People*. London: Orchard Books.

Sesame Street video about empathy: https://www.youtube.com/watch?v=9_1Rt1R4xbM

Empowerment

Canning, N. (2020) *The Significance of Children's Play and Empowerment: An Observational tool – TACYYC*. Occasional Paper 14. https://oro.open.ac.uk/69377/1/TACTYC%20OCC-Paper-14-N-Canning.pdf

Planning for Empowerment – Australian Government: https://www.earlychildhoodaustralia.org.au/wp-content/uploads/2021/08/Be-You-Planning-for-Empowerment-Digital.pdf

For children

Stories of real-life children being kind and activists: Kirby, L. (2022) *Do Something for Someone Else*. London: Magic Cat Publishing.

Familiarity

The Importance of Routine in Childhood Blog: https://melbourne childpsychology.com.au/blog/the-importance-of-routine-in-childhood/

Mainstone-Cotton, S. (2020) *Supporting Children Through Change and Everyday Transitions: Practical Strategies for Practitioners and Parents*. London: Jessica Kingsley Publishers.

Forgiveness

Helping Children Understand Forgiveness Blog: https://littlesunshine.com/helping-children-understand-forgiveness/

For children

Powerful message about forgiveness: Na'ima, R. (2020) *Let It Go: Learning the Lesson of Forgiveness*. Leicester: The Islamic Foundation. What Is Forgiveness for Children video: https://www.youtube.com/watch?v=FFuHL6Izk6E

Generosity

Tips for Raising Generous Children Blog: https://childmind.org/article/tips-for-raising-generous-children/

For children

This story is about sharing and community: Mora, O. (2018) *Thank You, Omu!* New York: Little, Brown Young Readers US.

Gentleness

The American Psychological Association Blog on Teaching About Gentleness: https://www.apa.org/topics/parenting/teaching-kids-gentleness

Interesting information about the gentle teaching approach from a Residential Special School in Kent: https://www.bradstow.wandsworth.sch.uk/624/gentle-teaching

For children

This is a lift-the-flap book which shows children sharing and doing kind things for each other: Campbell Books (2022) *I Like to Be Kind*. London: Campbell Books. This is part of a series in which Janet Rose (Emotion Coaching UK and Norland College) shares her expertise for parents/adults.

Hold in mind

The Birth to 5 Matters section on *Attachment and the role of the key person* Talks About Holding Children in Mind: https://birthto5matters.org.uk/attachment-and-the-role-of-the-key-person/

Blog post written by Tamsin, published by Parenta: https://www.parenta.com/2021/06/01/meaningful-connections-full-of-love/

Read, V. (2014) *Developing Attachment in Early Years Settings: Nurturing Secure Relationships from Birth to Five Years*. 2nd edn. Abingdon: Routledge.

Inclusive

Inclusive Practice and Equalities Section in Birth to 5 Matters: https://birthto5matters.org.uk/inclusive-practice-and-equalities/
Payne, K. (2022) *Supporting the Wellbeing of Children with SEND.* Abingdon: Routledge.

For children

Rhyming book about how we all have equal value: Davies, B. and Martin, F. (2023) *No Matter What . . . We All Belong.* London: Little Tiger Press Ltd.
Story about welcoming others into our community: Kefford, N. and Moore, L. (2010) *When the Dragons Came.* London: Simon and Schuster.
Story exploring exclusive play using the example of a big box: Rosen, M. (2007) *This Is Our House.* London: Walker Books.
Story promoting inclusion and acceptance: Kemp, A. (2010) *Dogs Don't Do Ballet.* London: Simon & Schuster.

Independence

Bryce-Clegg, A. (2013) *50 Fantastic Ideas for Promoting Independence.* London: Featherstone.
Levine, A. and Philips, L. (2023) *How to Build Independence in Preschoolers.* https://childmind.org/article/how-to-build-independence-in-preschoolers/

For children

Story about believing in yourself: Percival, T. (2021) *Tilda Tries Again*. London: Bloomsbury Children's Books.
Story about stepping out of your comfort zone and self-efficacy: Bright, R. (2017) *The Koala Who Could*. London: Orchard Books.

Joy

Blog about the *Role of Joy in Child Development*: https://www.miracle-recreation.com/blog/importance-of-joy-child-development/?lang=can
Kingston-Hughes, B. (2024) *Why Children Need Joy: The Fundamental Truth About Childhood* London: Sage.

For children

Laugh out loud with this story – it will help you feel joyful!: Fletcher, T. (2013) *The Dinosaur That Pooped a Planet*. Achill Island: Red Fox.
Story encouraging us to take pleasure in everyday moments: Witek, J. (2013) *All My Treasures: A Book of Joy*. Paris: De La Martinière Jeunesse.

Kindness

Blog about kindness in Early Childhood Education: https://www.housmaninstitute.com/blog/kindness-in-early-childhood-education

For children

Exploring kindness through a classroom incident: Miller, P. (2020) *Be Kind*. London: Pan Macmillan.

Exploring the power of a smile: Witek, J. (2013) *When I Smile: A Book of Kindness*. Paris: De La Martinière Jeunesse.

'Kindness Is Contagious' YouTube videos: https://www.youtube.com/watch?v=UyeP0XJQzjo&list=PL40c9F6JnVcj08KS1LvwSjaYiHriMLN1D

Story about being kind and generous to others: Pfister, M. (2007) *The Rainbow Fish*. New York: North South Books.

Thinking about how our behaviour affects others: McCloud, C. (2013) *Have You Filled a Bucket Today?* New York: Nelson Publishing.

Listening

Clark, A. and Moss, P. (2017) *Listening to Young Children: A Guide to Understanding and Using the Mosaic Approach*. London: Jessica Kingsley Publishers.

Mainstone-Cotton, S. (2019) *Listening to Young Children in Early Years Settings*. London: Jessica Kingsley Publishers.

For children

Chapman, G. (1992) *The 5 Love Languages: The Secret to Love that Lasts*. Chicago, IL: Northfield Publishing.

Chapman, G. and Campbell, R. (2012) *The 5 Love Languages of Children*. Chicago, IL: Northfield Publishing.

Chapman, G. and Freed, D. (2015) *Discovering the 5 Love Languages at School*. Chicago, IL: Northfield Publishing.

Exploring how it feels when things go wrong and how listening to others can help: Doerrfeld, C. (2020) *The Rabbit Listened*. London: Scallywag Press.

Love Languages (Words of Affirmation, Quality Time, Gifts, Touch and Acts of Service): https://5lovelanguages.com/

For children

Thinking about how we can love others through sharing time, baking, helping, etc.: Witek, J. (2013) *My Little Gifts: A Book of Sharing*. Paris: De La Martinière Jeunesse.

Nurture

Bradbury, A. and Grimmer, T. (2024) *Love and Nurture in the Early Years*. London: Sage.

Patience

Blog about the Importance of Patience in Childcare: https://www.thefoundationforlearning.com/child-care-glastonbury/the-importance-of-patience-in-child-care/

Blog about Teaching Patience to Children: https://www.scholastic.com/parents/family-life/social-emotional-learning/social-skills-for-kids/teaching-patience.html

For children

Book exploring patience aimed at young children: Campbell Books (2022) *Little Big Feelings Collection – I Can Be Patient*. London:

Campbell Books. This is part of a series in which Janet Rose (Emotion Coaching UK and Norland College) shares her expertise for parents/adults.

Professional love

Page, J. (2008) Permission to Love them. In Nutbrown, C. and Page, J. (Eds), *Working with Babies and Young Children from Birth to Three.* London: Sage, pp. 192–196.

Page, J. (2011) Do mothers want professional carers to love their babies? *Journal of Early Childhood Research*, 9(3), 310–323.

Page, J. (2014) Developing 'professional love' in early childhood settings. In Harrison, L. and Sumsion, J. (Eds), *Lived Spaces of Infant-Toddler Education and Care – Exploring Diverse Perspectives on Theory, Research, Practice and Policy.* Volume 11. International Perspectives on Early Childhood Education and Development Series. London: Springer Publishing, pp. 119–130.

Page, J. (2017) Reframing infant-toddler pedagogy through a lens of professional love: Exploring narratives of professional practice in early childhood settings in England. *Contemporary Issues in Early Childhood*, 18(4), 387–399.

Page, J. (2018) Characterising the principles of professional love in early childhood care and education. *International Journal of Early Years Education*, 26(2), 125–141.

https://research.brighton.ac.uk/en/persons/jools-page

For children

Explaining attachment as if it were an invisible string connecting us to the people we love: Karst, P. (2001) *The Invisible String.* Camarillo: Devorss Publishers.

Story exploring love and being loved: McBratney, S. and Jeram, A. (2009) *Guess How Much I Love Uou?* London: Walker Books.

Thinking about how we feel in our hearts when we experience different emotions: Witek, J. (2013) *In My Heart: A Book of Feelings*. Paris: De La Martinière Jeunesse.

Relationship and friendship

Information about relationships as part of the Early Years Foundation Stage: https://help-for-early-years-providers.education.gov.uk/personal-social-and-emotional-development/relationships

For children

Story exploring the joys and difficulties of making friends: Percival, T. (2019) *Meesha Makes Friends*. London: Bloomsbury Children's Books.

Respect

Article by the Children and Young People's Commissioner Scotland about respecting the human rights of very young children: https://rb.gy/tbqyqc

For children

Story about two monsters who have to respect each other's point of view: McKee, D. (2009) *Two Monsters*. London: Andersen Press.

Responsive

Handout from Responsive Caregiving Webinar, National Center on Early Childhood Development, Teaching and Learning, US: https://eclkc.ohs.acf.hhs.gov/sites/default/files/video/attachments/001764-baby-talks-handout.pdf

Safe and secure

Children's Right to Feel Safe: https://rights4children.org.uk/feeling-safe/
Siren Films videos about attachment, feeling safe and secure: https://www.sirenfilms.co.uk/library/attachment-feeling-safe-and-secure/

Safeguarding

Buckler, R. (2023) *Developing Child Centred Practice for Safeguarding and Child Protection.* Abingdon: Routledge.

Self-compassion

Neff, K. (2011) *Self Compassion.* London: Hodder & Stoughton.
Video about being kinder to yourself: https://www.youtube.com/watch?v=AyQdeYjXUhE
You can read some of Dr Neff's work around self-compassion on her website: https://self-compassion.org

Self-esteem

Neff, K. (2011) *Self Compassion*. London: Hodder & Stoughton.
Smith, J. (2022) *Why Has Nobody Told Me This Before*. London: Penguin.

For children

Story about perseverance and resilience: Bright, R. (2020) *Wobblysaurus*. London: Orchard Books.

Self-regulation

Education Endowment Foundation Section on Self-Regulation: https://educationendowmentfoundation.org.uk/early-years-evidence-store/self-regulation-and-executive-function
Grimmer, T. and Geens, W. (2022) *Nurturing Self-Regulation in Early Childhood*. Abingdon: Routledge.
Video About Self-Regulation and Co-Regulation. https://www.youtube.com/watch?v=RRMBHQ-Bmk0

For children

Exploring getting angry and emotional outbursts: Percival, T. (2019) *Ravi's Roar*. London: Bloomsbury Children's Books.
Exploring overwhelming feelings and frustration: Bright, R. (2022) *The Stompysaurus*. London: Orchard Books.
Helping children express their feelings: Cain, J. (2021) *The Way I Feel*. Chicago: Parenting Press.

Touch

All-Party Parliamentary Group on a Fit and Healthy Childhood (APPG) (2020) *Wellbeing and Nurture: Physical and Emotional Security in Childhood.* https://fhcappg.org.uk/wp-content/uploads/2020/07/ReportWellbeingandNurtureFinal140720.pdf

Piper, H. and Smith, H. (2003) 'Touch' in educational and child care settings: Dilemmas and responses. *British Educational Research Journal*, 29(6), 879–894.

For children

This rhyming book explores consent at children's level: Barkla, C. and Lee, J. (2022) *From My Head to My Toes, I Say What Goes*. Victoria, Australia: Bright Light.

Unconditional love

Grimmer, T. (2021) *Developing a Loving Pedagogy in Early Years.* Abingdon: Routledge.

For children

Explaining attachment as if it were an invisible string connecting us to the people we love: Karst, P. (2001) *The Invisible String*. Camarillo: Devorss Publishers.

Voice of the child

Clark, A. and Moss, P. (2017) *Listening to Young Children: A Guide to Understanding and Using the Mosaic Approach.* London: Jessica Kingsley Publishers.

United Nations Convention on the Rights of the Child: www.unicef.org.uk/Documents/Publication-pdfs/UNCRC_PRESS200910web.pdf

For children

Beautifully illustrated version of children's rights: Castle, C. (2001) *For Every Child: The UN Convention on the Rights of the Child.* London: Red Fox.

Warmth

Grimmer, T. (2021) *Developing a Loving Pedagogy in Early Years.* Abingdon: Routledge.

Wellbeing

Anxiety UK: https://www.anxietyuk.org.uk/

Chatterjee, R. (2018) *The Stress Solution the 4 Steps to a Calmer, Happier, Healthier You.* London: Penguin.

Mainstone-Cotton, S. (2017) *Promoting Emotional Wellbeing in Early Years Staff.* London: Jessica Kingsley Publishers.

Mainstone-Cotton, S. (2023) *Creativity and Wellbeing in Early the Years.* Abingdon: Routledge.

Siraj, I., Kingston, D. and Melhuish, E. (2024) *The Sustained Shared Thinking and Emotional Wellbeing Scale (SSTEW) Scale*. Abingdon: Routledge.

For children

Exploring feelings of anxiety and worry: Bright, R. (2020) *Worrysaurus*. London: Orchard Books.

Story about sharing our worries: Percival, T. (2018) *Ruby's Worry*. London: Bloomsbury Books.

Story about soothing anxiety: Morrisroe, R. (2022) *The Drama Llama*. London: Puffin.

Part 1 of this book provided an overview of many different aspects of a loving pedagogy. I hope it was able to offer some clarity around words and terms that can sometimes appear confusing.

This section of the book looks at how we can embed a loving pedagogy into our daily work. It will offer some practical ideas and suggestions. The areas this section is looking at are:

- The rights of the child in relation to a loving pedagogy;
- The importance of knowing what we believe – our professional identity;
- How to write a loving pedagogy policy;
- Reflecting upon our loving pedagogy;
- What adopting a loving pedagogy means in terms of relationships;
- How a loving pedagogy links to supporting behaviour;
- The implications of adopting a loving pedagogy for our safeguarding practices;
- What adopting a loving pedagogy means in terms of creating an enabling environment;
- How we can nurture our children through developing a loving pedagogy;
- How we can engage parents and work in partnership with them in relation to a loving pedagogy;
- Staff training and development.

The rights of the child in relation to loving pedagogy

The UN Convention on the Rights of the Child[10] is the main source of information about children's rights. This legally binding agreement consists of 54 articles which explain the rights of children. Since 1989, when the United Nations adopted it, 196 countries have signed, which means, for those countries, children's rights are enshrined in international law. The UK signed the convention in 1990, and it came into force in January 1992.

Upholding children's rights forms part of a loving approach; however, several articles appear particularly relevant when considering a loving pedagogy. The wording in the following articles is adapted from the children's version of the UNCRC:[73]

- **Article 2** – Non-discrimination
  Every child has all these rights, no matter who they are, where they live, what language they speak, what their religion is, what they think, what they look like, if they are a boy or girl, if they have a disability, if they are rich or poor, and no matter who their parents or families are or what their parents or families believe or do. No child should be treated unfairly for any reason.
- **Article 3** – The best interests of the child
  When adults make decisions, they should think about how their decisions will affect children. All adults should do what is best for children. Governments should make sure children are protected and looked after by their parents or by other people when this is needed and they should make sure that people and places responsible for looking after children are doing a good job.
- **Article 12** – Respect for children's views
  Children have the right to give their opinions freely on issues that affect them. Adults should listen and take children seriously.

DOI: 10.4324/9781003510529-51   **123**

- **Article 13** – Freedom of expression
  Children have the right to share freely with others what they learn, think and feel by talking, drawing, writing or using other methods unless it harms other people.
- **Article 14** – Freedom of thought, conscience and religion
  Children can choose their own thoughts, opinions and religion, but this should not stop other people from enjoying their rights. Parents can guide children so that as they grow up, they learn to use this right properly.
- **Article 23** – Disabled children
  Every child with a disability should enjoy the best possible life in society. Governments should remove all obstacles for children with disabilities so they can become independent and able to participate actively in the community.
- **Article 28** – Access to education
  Every child has the right to an education. Primary education should be free. Secondary and higher education should be available to every child. Children should be encouraged to go to school to the highest level possible. Discipline in schools should respect children's rights and never use violence.
- **Article 29** – Education and children's development
  Children's education should help them fully develop their personalities, talents and abilities. It should teach them to understand their own rights and to respect other people's rights, cultures and differences. It should help them to live peacefully and protect the environment.
- **Article 30 –** Minority culture, language and religion
  Children have the right to use their own language, culture and religion – even if these are not shared by most people in the country where they live.
- **Article 31** – Play and cultural and artistic activities
  Every child has the right to rest, relax, play and take part in cultural and creative activities.
- **Article 39** – Recovery from trauma and reintegration
  Children have the right to get help if they have been hurt, neglected, treated badly or affected by war so they can get back their health and dignity.

You can find more information about children's rights on the UNICEF website[74]. UNICEF also has an excellent children's book, *For Every Child*,[75] explaining these rights to children.

The importance of knowing what we believe – our professional identity

Our professional identity is about knowing what we value is important about young children's learning and development and why we believe these things. Love and a loving pedagogy needs to form part of this professional identity. Articulating our vision and values is vitally important because it helps us to share our thinking and, hopefully, encourage others to view children in this way. As practitioners, how we view children and our image of the child will underpin our pedagogical approach and values and this approach acts as a foundation for everything we do!

We should be evangelists for what we believe, striving to spread the word and our viewpoint – and if we don't know what we think – get thinking! It's not OK to sit on the fence. As practitioners, we must have a view – because you may have heard the phrase, "If you don't stand for something, you'll fall for anything!" To a certain extent, this is true. If we haven't worked out our own view – how will we know if the views of someone else fit within what we think and our ethos? As experts in early childhood education, we must use our knowledge about children and child development as the lens through which we view new information, for example, when we are faced with the next strategy or governmental guidance.

REFLECTION POINT – WHAT DO YOU BELIEVE?

I have written my own personal creed – which states clearly what I believe about young children and childhood and frames a loving pedagogy. These are my thoughts:

- Firstly, and most importantly, I believe that children should be loved.
- Children need to grow and develop in relationships with others.
- Children are competent, capable and rich in potential.
- Children are important in their own right and should have a recognised place in society as a group in themselves. I believe childhood to be a vitally important phase in our lives.
- Children can and do make a positive contribution and should be valued and listened to.
- Children should be allowed to play, be free to explore and investigate, and be given time to do so.
- Children should be respected, protected and kept safe whilst being allowed to take risks and be challenged as they grow and develop.
- Children should be able to direct their own learning at times, and their views should be taken into consideration in their education.

I now invite you to write your own personal creed. To state clearly what you believe about young children and childhood and why.

When our values and beliefs about young children lead our practice, it will be the foundation upon which we can base our whole provision. So, I challenge you to consider these questions:

- What does our ethos say about our setting and our views of children and childhood?
- What pedagogies and principles are underpinning our practice?
- Does our day-to-day practice typically reflect our ethos?

In my view, a loving pedagogy is the appropriate approach to take when considering the education and care of very young children. I want to re-share a quote about love from the Bible[76] which I shared in my *Loving Pedagogy* book.[9] Could we use this to describe us and our approach towards the child?

> Love is patient, love is kind. It does not envy, it does not boast, it is not proud. It does not dishonour others, it is not self-seeking, it is not easily angered, it keeps no record of wrongs. Love does not delight in evil but rejoices with the truth. It always protects, always trusts, always hopes, always perseveres.
>
> Love never fails.

How to write a loving pedagogy policy

Once we have established what we believe, it is essential that we include this within a policy. I suggest settings have a standalone loving pedagogy policy, although some settings will include these ideas within their current policies, for example, as part of their safeguarding or behaviour policy. Many settings are replacing their behaviour policy with a relationships policy which encompasses their loving pedagogy alongside their relational approach to supporting behaviour. All our policies need to complement each other and not be contradictory, so when introducing a new policy, this is the ideal time to review our other policies.

When writing a policy, begin with stating what you believe and why, perhaps outlining the importance of attachments and building strong relationships. Then, describe your approach, being specific in terms of how you will put your loving pedagogy into practice. Give examples, particularly in relation to touch. What constitutes an appropriate touch in your setting? How will you ensure touch is consented to? What boundaries have you put in place? How are you safeguarding the children and staff?

You will want to consider involving the children in some way when writing your policy. Perhaps adapting a mosaic approach to listen to them and ascertain their views about your provision. They need to be at the centre of the policy. It is also helpful to think about parents' views and how you will liaise with them, including a written statement about this. Lastly, a policy needs to be dated and have a review date specified so that you can plan to evaluate how well it is working.

DOI: 10.4324/9781003510529-53

Here are some statements that may be useful when formulating a policy:

- Children need to feel safe, secure, loved and a sense of belonging within their early childhood setting. We strive to nurture these feelings within our children through daily practice.
- We recognise that the welfare of children is paramount and will work in partnership with children, families, carers and other agencies to promote this.
- All children, regardless of age, disability, gender, racial or cultural heritage, religious belief, sexual orientation or identity, have the right to equal protection from all types of harm or abuse and a right to feel loved.
- We believe nurturing touch is vital to children's emotional, physical, cognitive and social development and we will use positive nurturing touch in our practice. For example, children may sit on adult's laps, adults will hold children's hands or we may praise a child by ruffling their hair or offering them a high-five.
- We will always take immediate action if it is felt that there has been any inappropriate use of touch within the setting, and the setting's Safeguarding and Child Protection Policy will be followed.
- Loving and nurturing practices are an essential part of building relationships and secure attachments.
- We strive to build close emotional relationships between children and key people or other members of staff.
- We believe that each child has the unique ability to achieve and succeed during their time with us.
- We will support every child according to their individual needs and adapt our approach according to the age and developmental stage of each child.
- We demonstrate love to our children through:
  - Physical expressions of love such as cuddles, holding hands, kissing hurts better;
  - Meeting children's personal care needs with dignity and respect;
  - Offering guidance and boundaries to keep them safe;
  - Providing emotional warmth;

- Promoting children's interests and keeping them central to our practice;
- Safeguarding and protecting them;
- Giving our children and accepting from them love tokens or gifts, for example, a feather, conker or pebble;
- Accepting and reciprocating their expressions of love towards us;
- Holding children in mind when we are not with them.

Reflecting upon our loving pedagogy

I believe critical reflection[77] to be a valuable professional development tool which can help us to improve our practice over time, think about what we do and why we do it and generally develop our teaching and what we do as practitioners. Critical reflection involves skills such as analysis and reflection and many theorists[78,79,80] have written extensively about this topic both within education as a whole and also within Early Childhood Education.[81,82]

When reflecting upon our work with children, there will always be a practical element and impact because critical reflection questions our assumptions and why we do things the way we do and considers wider social issues in relation to our practices. Most importantly, when we critically reflect upon our practice, it should result in action in some way.[83] We need to reflect upon our loving pedagogy in the same way that we would reflect upon other aspects of our practice.

The following questions adapted from *Developing a Loving Pedagogy*[9] might help us reflect upon our loving pedagogy:

- How do we articulate our loving pedagogy and define "professional love"?
- Can we outline the interactions that make up our own loving pedagogy?
- What are our thoughts around love and intimacy, and how do we relate these to parents and carers?
- What do we say to reassure parents and carers who might not want us to "love" their children and address any safeguarding concerns they may have?
- To what extent have we discussed with colleagues how we interact physically with the children in our care and demonstrate love through touch?

- What impact will speaking our children's love languages have on their self-esteem, behaviour and attachment? How can we find this out?
- How can adults speak children's "love languages" more fluently?
- How do we ascertain the views of our children and see the world from their perspective?
- What examples can we share of being an advocate for the children in our care?
- What does "holding children in mind" look like in our setting?
- In what ways do we see our setting through our children's eyes?
- Could our setting be described as acting as a secure base for our children? How do we know?
- How do we foster a true sense of belonging in the place and space of our setting?
- Do practitioners feel able to demonstrate their love to the children in their care and how do they do this in a professional capacity?
- Do we have an ethos of permission with regard to acting in loving ways?
- What does our loving early years environment look like in practice?
- What is our first step in developing or further developing a loving pedagogy in our setting?

Another way of reflecting on our practice is to use a reflection tool and try to assess or measure the impact of our loving pedagogy. Often the areas we assess within our provision are seen as higher priorities. For example, if we audit opportunities for mark-making or counting within the environment, we often use these assessments to prioritise future funding or continued professional development (CPD). These things are important, of course; however, if we only measure things like whether or not a child can write their name or count to 10, we may miss measuring the more important things like if our children feel a sense of belonging and feel loved in our settings.

In our book *Love and Nurture in the Early Years*,[84] Aaron and I share an idea for developing a child-centred approach which reflects upon children and their sense of belonging in our setting. It is called the "Child in the NOW" model. We invite practitioners to reflect upon their practice and review different aspects of their provision in the light of the model, as seen in the text box that follows.

CHILD IN THE NOW MODEL[84]

Figure 2.1 Child in the NOW model

Source: (Adapted from Bradbury and Grimmer, 2024)

This model explores a child's sense of **belonging** (where they feel part of our group), **becoming** (children are constantly learning and developing), **being** (children developing a sense of self and in attuned relationships with others) and **believing** (when we advocate for children and believe in them and their capabilities). We explore these within four principles:

- **Learning Outcomes** – Reminds us as practitioners of our role to develop children's involvement in learning and self-confidence.
- **Early Years Practices** – Should be holistic, integrated, interconnected and play-based.
- **Relationships** – Secure, respectful and reciprocal.
- **Love and Nurture** – Meeting basic needs, expressing love and affection, ensuring children feel safe and secure.

A loving pedagogy is often seen within our practice, so this may be described as a grass-roots or bottom-up approach; however, our practice should be guided by policy. Imagine how amazing it would be if a top-down approach was also the most loving! I have recently met and been inspired by Jane Malcolm, who influenced the Scottish early years' national practice guidance *Realising the Ambition: Being Me*[85] (2020) and *The Promise Scotland*[86] (2020) by bringing love into policy. She has created a framework,[87] called love-led practice, and shares a little of her experiences in the text box that follows. This highlights how powerful it can be when love is embedded in policy. When I was involved in writing *Birth to 5 Matters*,[88] I was encouraged to read that love was represented within the document and, during the editing process, I proposed where the terms love and loving might fit in more places. I was thrilled that this wording was adopted into the final guidance; therefore, within England, we are moving in the same direction, at least through our non-statutory guidance.

LOVE-LED PRACTICE
JANE MALCOLM, MPHIL, UNIVERSITY OF EDINBURGH

In Scotland, love has become part of the language of working with children and young people with its inclusion in the policy documents *Realising the Ambition: Being Me*[85] and *The Promise Scotland*.[86] This wasn't always the case. When I first began my research,[87] practitioners said they loved the children they worked with but would never say that openly because they felt it was professionally inappropriate. No one could explain why other than to say that it wasn't in the "rules" as they didn't have policy or guidance to support them to express their feelings appropriately. However, my research into Scottish Early Learning and Childcare (ELC) policy showed that "love" wasn't forbidden, but it wasn't explicitly encouraged.

The authors of Realising the Ambition heard me challenge this and said, "It was vital that Realising the Ambition be based on research, evidence and current thinking. We were aware of Jane's work and were inspired by it and, as such, it added weight and justification to the inclusion of the concept of love within the national practice guidance of Scotland."

This was a huge turning point for love in Scottish ELC. Practitioners now had guidance permitting them to talk about love. Love became part of the professional language of ELC.

To support an understanding of how to ensure the language in guidance and policy reflected the language used by practitioners, I developed the concept of love-led practice[87] along with a reflective tool, The Framework for Love-Led Practice (the Framework). Love-led practice reflects the holistic nature of love in ELC, and the Framework offers a reflective tool in which practitioners can understand how to support love at the heart of the practice. The Framework comprises eight aspects of practice: Development, Intimacy, Security, Passion, Physical, Child's Love, Relationships and Workforce.

The purpose of the Framework is to help nurseries reflect upon the different aspects of practice and to consider if they are taking a loving approach in all aspects. There is not one aspect more important than another; reflecting upon them all will support love-led practice. Children have a right to experience love, and this Framework ensures that this is considered when developing love-led practice.

The Framework can be useful in several ways:

- It allows practitioners to talk about love.
- Encourages self-reflection on personal experiences of love and the impact on practice.
- Gives a focus on exploring leadership styles.
- Gives practitioners the language with which they can articulate and recognise loving practice.
- Provides a variety of ways in which loving practice can be explored.

What adopting a loving pedagogy means in terms of relationships

Part 1 of this book briefly explains attachment theory, and there are some suggestions for additional reading and resources in the middle section which might help if you want to explore this area further because relationships are central to a loving pedagogy, and an understanding of attachment theory is vital. There is a wealth of research[15,89,90] which reiterates the importance of relationships and the impact these relationships have on our personal, social and emotional development. In our book *Nurturing Self-regulation*,[59] Wendy and I talk about how self-regulation develops out of co-regulation, that is, where adults interact in the moment, coach and role-model instruction to scaffold children's learning. Co-regulation relies on the foundation of loving, responsive and secure attachments between adults and children.

Daniel Siegel and Tina Bryson[91] share some helpful ideas about attachment. They talk about the four S's: children need to feel safe, seen, soothed and secure:

- **Safe** – Make a commitment that we will never be a source of fear. This includes increasing children's cortisol levels, for example, through shaming, embarrassing them or judging them. We must also repair and restore relationships if needed; this will mean apologising for our mistakes and role modelling forgiveness.
- **Seen** – Notice the children and be curious about what they do and why. We can use our observations and knowledge of the children to make links with their lives, talk about things that are important to them and tap into their interests and fascinations.
- **Soothed** – Before situations arise where children can become dysregulated, help them to calm and de-escalate themselves. Seigel and Bryson talk about offering children our PEACE – Presence, Engagement, Affection, Calm and Empathy.

DOI: 10.4324/9781003510529-55

◦ **Secure** – Invest in a relational trust fund! Every time we are there for a child, it's as if we are investing in their relational trust fund. Build secure attachments with children so that they can view us and our relationship as a secure base.

These four S's contribute to a child's sense of belonging and sense of being in terms of their identity.

Building secure attachments with the children in our care is an important part of our role as caregivers and, from the moment our children arrive, we are in a relationship with them. Everything we do daily will either help or hinder the children's experiences of relationships. Bowlby[92] talks about how we create Internal Working Models (IWM), or blueprints, of what relationships are like based on these experiences. If we cannot rely on our caregivers, our IWM will be based on an insecure attachment and we won't necessarily know what positive and secure attachments can be like. Bowlby also suggested that we only need to experience one secure attachment to know what good relationships can be like. We can provide a secure attachment for the children in our care and, thus, enable them to have an IWM of a positive and reliable relationship.

When we spend time with the children, enjoy being with them and have fun playing, we will be a magnet for them. Our children will want to be with us and enjoy attending our setting. In turn, this increases our levels of brain chemicals such as Oxytocin and serotonin and enhances our relationships and bonds with the children. As these relationships develop, we will find that our children will respond positively to us. We may notice them demonstrating their love in a variety of ways and expressing their love languages, and our role is to respond sensitively and reciprocally to this.

SAYING, "I LOVE YOU!" – REFLECTIONS FROM A PRACTITIONER

I remember hearing a discussion between educators during some training I attended as a teacher as to what an appropriate response would be if a child tells you they love you. Lots of practitioners responded that "thank you, I like you too" or "that's lovely" would suffice. I was the only one who said I would reply with "I love you too," and, at the time, I was made to feel like this would be considered inappropriate. Particularly now, as a childminder, I have children in my setting who will soon be four who I have looked after since they were small babies. How could I not love them? They often tell me they love me, and I tell them I love them back because that's the truth, and surely that's the best environment for them to be in.

Saying, "I love you!" – Tamsin's thoughts

Children often tell us they love us nonverbally, for example, through gifts, cuddles or wanting to spend time with us, but sometimes they will use words. I am regularly asked what a practitioner should do if a child tells them they love them within a professional context.

My answer to this is twofold:

- Do you love the child?
- How might this fit within your policy?

Firstly, reflect upon whether or not you feel you can reciprocate in terms of depth of feeling. Do you actually love the child? Is this a word you feel comfortable in using? I do not think we should tell a child we love them if we do not. Having said that, many people use the word love very loosely and might say things like "love you guys" regularly. If you want to say I love you back, I personally do not have a problem with this, provided it fits within your policies in your setting.

Therefore, you also need to think about the content of your policies and your role within the setting. Have a discussion as a team about what you want the policy to include. If you are specific in your policies about your loving pedagogy, you can stand firm in this and this will help you know how to respond.

Potential responses to a child who says, "I love you!":

- "I love you too!"
- "Thank you. I love that you've said that to me!"
- Give them a love token . . . a special pebble/feather or a paper heart.

- "That is such a kind thing to say; it has made me feel really happy!"
- "Thank you for telling me – I feel really loved!"
- "Awww!" Smile, then offer to give them a hug.
- "You saying 'I love you' makes me feel special."
- "I love all the children here at XYZ setting . . ."
- Find out their love languages and respond in another love language appropriate to them.

How a loving pedagogy links to supporting behaviour

Adopting a loving pedagogy has implications for the way we respond to and support children with their behaviour. It is a relational approach based on attachment theory, which sees all behaviours as children communicating their needs and wants. Our response to children's behaviour needs to be one which attempts to discover the reasons why children behave the way they do so that we can be proactive, not reactive. In my book *Supporting Behaviour and Emotions*[28] I talk about becoming a behaviour detective and exploring these reasons.

Within schools and settings, we need to view behaviour differently. Rather than thinking in terms of "behaviour management" which views children as needing to be managed and controlled, we can think about behaviour as something to be learned and developed through positive experiences. Children are learning to behave, learning which behaviours are acceptable in particular circumstances or learning how to act and react when they experience specific emotions. Naturally, they will make behavioural learning mistakes, just like a child learning to form their letters correctly and occasionally writes a letter backwards or upside down. Therefore we need to practise acceptance of these mistakes and see them as the child learning, not chastise or tell the child off. Yes, they need to learn that it's not OK to hurt others when they are angry, for example, but we can teach this without resorting to punishment or negative sanctions. We wouldn't dream of telling a child who wrote their name backwards to sit on a step for five minutes and think about what they have done! Yet, for some reason, with behavioural mistakes, we treat them differently and have, sometimes, unrealistic expectations which set children up to fail and do not support their learning.

DOI: 10.4324/9781003510529-56

We should be inclusive in our response to behaviour. Some children will require more support, additional resources or modifications to the space in order to be included. Everyone is not the same and cannot be treated as such, so being fair in our approach is not about treating everyone equally; it is about equity and treating everyone according to their individual needs. Having the same rules for everyone is not equitable at times; for example, if one child finds it very difficult to sit and listen to a five-minute story, to demand this of them could mean they fail and possibly disrupt others. Instead, having a lower time expectation for this child would be appropriate, and perhaps backward chaining, for example, inviting the child to join the story for the last minute so that they can be successful in listening to the story.

CHANGES TO POLICY

Many settings and schools are now reframing their "Behaviour Management" policy and making it a "Nurturing Self-regulation" policy, "Supporting Positive Behaviour" policy, "Relationships" policy or even (my favourite) writing it into a "Loving Pedagogy" policy. What follows are some extracts from some policies which I hope will be helpful to read. (As policies are reviewed regularly, wording can change; however, these were correct at the time of writing.)

Extracts from Conewood Children's Centre – Loving pedagogy statement

Conewood Children's Centre holds the Loving Pedagogy at the centre of its curriculum. It is interwoven with our trauma-sensitive approach that actively seeks to build stronger brains by tipping the scale for positive success. To be successful for every child, we remain curious, understanding and responsive using the methodologies described. We also know that for children to learn best, they need to feel safe, secure and trusted. This happens when our brains produce positive hormones like Oxytocin and are not flooded with constant toxic stress hormones.

This is Professional Love.

Love languages

We recognise the value in identifying children's predominant way of showing their love language so that we foster stronger connections and attachment with each child. We also see this as part of each child's story, enabling us to understand "how it feels to be me" truly.

We seek to respond to each child's love language by offering back a serve and return interaction that connects with each "Love language." In this way, we are holding the child in mind and present this to them as an acknowledgement they will appreciate.

Understanding behaviour

The heart of supporting a child who may find regulation more challenging is based on understanding. Whether that is through knowing their story or being tuned in to predict a challenge, it all comes back to understanding. Behaviours are there to tell you something, and using the Loving Pedagogy, we believe it is our job to hear and comprehend these stories.

Reframing language

By embedding the Loving Pedagogy into our approach, we must remember the importance of the words and language we use. Frequently, we hear descriptions of children's behaviour that can invoke a negative connotation. When we think about the phrases "Having a tantrum" or "Attention-seeking," our unconscious thoughts immediately lead us to believe these are negative.

Instead, we aim to use language that avoids disapproval and promotes understanding. When we make an observation that a behaviour may be "Attachment seeking" or appropriate for the brain development of a 2-year-old, we then remove judgement and replace this with the understanding to support the child's need.

Extracts from Balham Nursery School – Relationship and behaviour policy

Relationships and attachment

At Balham Nursery, we value the strong relationships we have with children and their families. A child's Key Person will endeavour to have a secure attachment with each of their key children. Children have the right to feel safe and secure in order to learn. Strong adult-child relationships are built through emotion coaching (co-regulation in practice) in order to help children develop the skills they need to be able to self-regulate.

Rewards

At Balham Nursery School, we want children to be driven by internal motivation, the satisfaction of doing the right thing, rather than a tangible reward such as a sticker. We do not use stickers or reward charts. Practitioners give children social rewards such as specific praise, a high five or telling other members of the team or their parents/carers.

Extracts from Willow and Archway Children's Centres "understanding and supporting positive behaviour" policy

At Willow and Archway Children's Centres, we believe that our trauma-informed practice with aspects of "Loving Pedagogy" enables children to develop a positive self-image, have high self-esteem and become confident. We believe that we all do best when our personal social and emotional needs are met and where there are clear and appropriate expectations for behaviour. We want the children to respect and feel respected by children and adults. It is therefore very important to recognise when there is a "need," understand it, label the emotion, express it and support children to regulate. The children will begin to develop an understanding of acceptable behaviour and the ability to empathise with others.

Children learn by example, so we ensure that our own behaviour is a good model for them. We give this policy to our staff and parents with the hope of ensuring that staff and parents are working together and are on the same page. We find this helps in ensuring children are given consistent messages about what is and is not expected of them. This, in turn, helps to make them feel safe.

Understanding and supporting positive behaviour

We believe that by understanding child development through the lens of neuroscience, we can support children to build strong, healthy

143

brains that enable them to grow in their resilience to becoming happy, healthy and successful individuals. Brain development is most rapid in the early years, and a good foundation is of crucial importance for children's development.

We understand that behaviours are a way for children to express what they want and need and how they feel. Behaviours are a way of communicating when we either do not have the words or cannot use them in the moment (sometimes when we are feeling strong feelings like anger or sadness).

Extracts from Somerset Nursery School – Relationship and positive behaviour policy

Children's behaviour is an expression and reflection of the experience, including their encounters with adults and other children. We believe that children learn good behaviour and respect through positive role models and need to be guided in that learning by sensitive supportive adults. It is our responsibility as adults working with young children to be aware of children's behaviour, to ensure their safety and to use all our resources to understand the processes that result in that behaviour.

The implications of adopting a loving pedagogy for our safeguarding practices

Adopting a loving pedagogy impacts every aspect of our provision. Warm, loving relationships can be misinterpreted by other people or deemed inappropriate if they do not understand our approach. In addition, a loving pedagogy involves using consented positive touch as part of daily practice; therefore, there are naturally some safeguards that need to be put in place to ensure children and staff are kept free from abuse, ill-treatment or suspicion of abuse or ill-treatment. We need to take consent seriously and nurture a culture of consent from the outset. Part 1 of this book considers both safeguarding and consent, and additional ideas are provided in the further reading and resources section.

EXTRACTS FROM POLICIES IN RELATION TO SAFEGUARDING

From a childminding setting. Although childminders do not need written policies, this childminder shared how she wanted to write them down to ensure her policies and procedures were transparent and clear:

> *My first responsibility and priority will always be to the children in my care. I always offer children appropriate physical contact according to their age and stage of development. My setting is a warm and caring environment where I cuddle babies, hug children and kiss bumps on the head better! I believe that loving physical contact is vital for a child's wellbeing.*

From Conewood Children's Centre

Together as a Team, we have gained consensus and agreed on the following:

(Please note that we hold our Safeguarding Duties and responsibilities extremely seriously and the safeguarding of our children is our foremost and highest priority.)

- Physical Touch: Holding a child's hand, stroking their arm, gentle squeezes up and down the arms (as a sensory response) are all ways that we will show that we care for our children.
- Kisses: Blowing an air kiss is an appropriate response. The act of giving an actual kiss to a child is something we do not do. We do not use the "kiss it better" approach, although we may, where appropriate, encourage a child to blow a kiss onto their own minor injuries.
- Cuddles: This is very much a part of the way that we show that we care at Conewood and we will offer cuddles to children if and when they need them. Children will be asked "Do you want a cuddle" first with respect and dignity, allowing the child to give their consent. We will not give cuddles if a child says no, and we will not ask a child to "Give me a cuddle." Cuddles are only ever given in open spaces where other adults are nearby.
- When a child tells you they "love you." We would acknowledge the comment and respond with a phrase that may state, "I really like being with you too, how lovely," or a diluted response such as "I really love you coming to nursery, too." We wouldn't directly say "I love you, too" in response.
- Sitting on laps: We do allow children to sit on our lap but will only allow babies and younger children to sit front facing when it is part of soothing or rocking children to sleep.
- Face contact: Younger babies may be held cheek to cheek for soothing and comfort. However, we will not blow raspberries, tickle a child or rub noses.

- Hair and earrings: We recognise the cultural importance and respect that must be given to each child's hair. We will replace hair ties/clips that have come loose, and we may also speak to parents about tying a child's hair up if it is interfering with their activities. Touching or stroking a child's hair would only be done if they gave their consent. If a child's earrings become loose, they will be returned in an envelope.

It is our policy to always ask for a child's consent "Can I change your nappy?," "Can I blow your nose?" We see this as respecting the child, their voice and their choice. We work with the child to ensure that it's their permission that determines the way we approach an action. Children can give consent using words, their body language and their behaviour.

What adopting a loving pedagogy means in terms of creating an enabling environment

An enabling environment within a loving pedagogy is enabling the child holistically, physically, cognitively, socially, emotionally, spiritually and in a way that promotes their mental and intellectual growth. A truly enabling environment would do this because it would enable all aspects of a child and their development. When we plan our environment, we often think about covering, for example, curriculum areas, like the seven areas of learning and development in the Early Years Foundation Stage; however, it can help to look beyond this and think in broader terms. Is our environment supporting children's mental health or emotional wellbeing? Is it promoting a sense of awe and wonder or children's spiritual development? Can we look deeply at both our indoor and outdoor provision and consider the opportunities for loving interactions?

A loving and enabling environment is an ethos which:

- Keeps the child central to our provision;
- Promotes a child's holistic development;
- Taps into children's interests and fascinations;
- Prioritises wellbeing and emotional intelligence;
- Ensures children and their families are represented and see themselves within the environment;
- Promotes children's independence and autonomy;
- Includes all children and removes barriers to participation;
- Advocates for children's rights and affords children agency;
- Empowers children and families;
- Encompasses compassion and forgiveness within our interactions;
- Practises consented-to positive touch.

DOI: 10.4324/9781003510529-58

In practical terms, a loving and enabling environment will be one which engages children in learning by providing exciting and stimulating resources, inviting provocations and is accessible to all. Having a calm area or safe space can be helpful when encouraging children to feel like they belong. Creating areas like this can be simple and very effective. When I was child-minding, I used to put a blanket over my dining table and then put cushions underneath, and the children used to love hiding in the makeshift den! Sometimes my children used to use our clothes horse in this way too, by using clothes pegs to clip a cloth over it and then spend hours in their secret hideout!

AN ENABLING ENVIRONMENT – A CHILDMINDER'S VIEW

I try to make my learning environment feel like a second home for the children in my care. I created this calming area by using a travel cot on its side and filling it with soft blankets, cushions and resources that I know my children will be interested in. Children can use these spaces as a den, quiet space or calming area. I have even had a child use it for a nap!

Our learning environment will have a huge impact on our children's emotional wellbeing. We must ensure it feels welcoming and inclusive and enables children to feel safe and secure. Having consistent routines, good organisation and predictable expectations can also help with a sense of familiarity and safety. This is particularly important if we have any children from chaotic or disorganised homes, or children with insecure attachments, as they may feel anxious or live with constant uncertainty. We can ensure our settings are counter to this and soothe children through our calm atmosphere. In simple terms, this can mean removing broken resources and replacing tatty or ripped displays because, to a certain extent, how we care for our learning environment can be seen as a reflection of our loving ethos. This can give a powerful message to not only visitors to the setting, such as prospective parents, but also to our children about our love for them. Being proud of our learning environment instils pride in our whole provision, which rubs off on others.

How we can nurture our children through developing a loving pedagogy

A loving pedagogy nurtures children and enables them to grow and develop. In our book[47] about this topic, as shared in Part 1, Aaron and I compare nurturing a child to tending a garden,

> Often the phrase lovingly nurtured is used when thinking about tending to a garden which implies a longer-term commitment. To lovingly nurture our children, we meet their immediate needs with a long-term view, just as we might nurture a seed, knowing that we are helping a plant or flower to grow. Our focus is broadly on the bigger picture; however, we still need to manage the detail as we feed and water the seedling and make sure the environment offers enough light and nutrients daily for it to grow.
>
> (p. 24)

To nurture someone is to care for them as they are developing or growing and it could be argued that nurture and love are inseparable and interconnected. We cannot love someone without nurturing them, and when we nurture someone, it is, by its very essence, loving. We also cannot nurture in isolation from each other. Nurturing is about connection and relationships. When we nurture children, we build relationships, promote children's self-esteem and self-worth and provide opportunities for children to thrive in our care.

There are many ways we can nurture our children through love:

- Creating secure attachments and relationships;
- Being kind, caring and loving in our actions and words;
- Communicating honestly and openly together;
- Speaking our children's love languages;
- Practising compassion, acceptance and forgiveness;

DOI: 10.4324/9781003510529-59

- Supporting our children emotionally and co-regulating them as they develop self-regulation;
- Being empathetic and role-modelling empathy;
- Supporting children through transitions;
- Helping children to feel safe and secure;
- Having developmentally appropriate expectations;
- Promoting children's wellbeing.

NURTURING AND EMPOWERING CHILDREN – WILLOW CHILDREN'S CENTRE

We help to support children's self-esteem by enabling them to be successful in play experiences and activities. We organise both the indoor and outdoor learning environment so it meets the needs of the children and provides appropriate challenges.

In a forest school session, child S felt empowered to jump from the mossy bank, which demonstrates how our nurturing ethos empowered them.

We encourage children and nurture them through their play, help-ing them to set appropriate goals and challenges. We praise them every time we see children taking any steps towards a new skill. Hearing the praise will really encourage them to keep going in that direction. In one session, through our encouragement, child A felt able to climb the climbing wall independently.

How we can engage parents and work
in partnership with them in relation
to a loving pedagogy

It is vital that we include parents and carers in adopting a loving pedagogy. Parents are the child's first educators and not only experts in their children but experts in *loving* their children. We can learn so much from working closely with them. In addition, we can share our knowledge and ideas about attachment and love languages with parents, which may enhance their relationship with their children.

Our policies or mission statement will probably include our ethos in relation to working with families, and it is imperative that they feel included and welcomed in our provision. We want our parents to know that their children's wellbeing and happiness are of vital importance, and we want their child to feel at home and that they belong in our setting. We will endeavour to engage with and work in partnership with parents to ensure their children's emotional needs are met. The key person in a setting plays an important role and is best placed to build professional relationships with families.

We can cultivate a welcoming ethos and engage parents through:

- Sharing our loving pedagogy from day one;
- Reassuring parents of our love and care for their child;
- Earning parents' trust by being honest, authentic and respectful;
- Getting to know children and families really well, learning and using their names and asking about their lived experiences;
- Building secure attachments with children and families;
- Helping children feel safe and secure through familiar routines, consistent expectations and boundaries and reliable, trustworthy relationships;
- Supporting children and parents through any transitions: vertical – into or out of the setting; or between rooms, and horizontal – throughout the daily routine;
- Sharing knowledge of their child's learning and development.

DOI: 10.4324/9781003510529-60

A PARENT'S VIEW

A parent's view – Westbourne Children's Centre

Westbourne Children's Centre has adopted a loving pedagogy and shared a loving pedagogy statement with families. They received lots of positive comments and feedback about adopting this approach, including the following email from a parent:

"Thanks so much for sending this through – incredibly helpful, and I feel very pleased E is in an environment which wants to press into this approach. Thanks so much for this!"

A parent's view – Preschool setting

"When we chose which preschool for our child to attend, we deliberately looked for a setting which felt really loving. We also wanted a play-based setting where our child would be given freedom to learn through play. Our child settled in really well and we are certain this is because of the relationship our daughter made with 'Miss Sandy' and the other adults. We could relax because we knew our daughter was loved and happy."

A parent's view – Childminder

"I love all the children in my care and tell the parents this when they come for a look around. I think this intimate feel is partly why parents choose my setting, alongside the 'home-from-home' feel. Parents often comment on our cosy spaces and how it feels like their children are at a friend or family member's home for the day."

Staff training and development

There are many ways that we can remain up-to-date and current in terms of our loving pedagogy. What follows are some ideas of how we can continue to develop our practice.

Observing each other – Peer observations can be helpful in terms of highlighting effective practice and learning from colleagues. Sometimes, having a focus for the observations can help, for example, asking a colleague to observe how you use touch within a session or noting your use of different love languages.

Inset and training – I work with settings and deliver training and inset about loving pedagogy, and I have colleagues who also deliver training in this area. Having said this, and without wanting to do myself out of a job (!) you could work through my book or use the various material available about loving pedagogy to lead your own training event.

Staff meetings – In our staff meetings, we can allow time for discussion about practice and reflect on our practice together. These meetings are an invaluable time when we can all have input into the way we work, share ideas and problem-solve together. I know some settings that have focused on touch and thought in detail about how they do and intend to use touch in their practice. Discussing this in the staff meeting ensured that everyone's voice was heard.

Audits and self-evaluation – In a similar way, we can use audits and self-evaluation to review our practice together. Usually self-evaluation consists of a series of questions that you discuss as a team, then noting your strengths and any areas for development, turning these into an action plan. I have shared a self-evaluation proforma on my website, which asks a series of questions and invites practitioners to reflect upon their practice in the light of a loving pedagogy. In addition, you might choose to use audits such as the Sustained Shared Thinking and

Emotional Wellbeing scale (SSTEW),[93] which is an early childhood environmental rating scale along the same line as the Early Childhood Environment Rating Scale (ECERS)[94] and the Infant/Toddler Environment Rating Scale (ITERS).[95] These are used by practitioners and researchers reading the quality statements (which go from inadequate to excellent) and equating them to their practice; this then "rates" their provision, giving it a score.

Reviewing policies and procedures – Another way that we can develop our practice is to review our policies and procedures in the light of our loving pedagogy. In a setting, the policies should outline what we intend to do and how we intend to do things, and our procedures are what we actually do to follow these policies. Our practice should align with this; however, sometimes, our day-to-day practices are slightly different from our policies. Therefore, it is essential that we review our policies as well as our procedures and ensure that both are in line with what we do.

Discussing our practice with children, families and other stakeholders – This ensures everyone's views are represented and helps us receive feedback about our practice. Sharing what we do with families can also help them in their relationships with the children. For example, talking to parents about consent might raise some important issues that have otherwise not been discussed or considered by parents.

I have a wealth of information on my website[96] about a loving pedagogy and training on subjects that overlap or link are delivered by organisations such as Early Education[97] and Early Excellence.[98] In addition, Kathy Brodie regularly has speakers on Early Years TV[99] covering subjects that link with a loving pedagogy. There are also a number of platforms, such as Kinderly,[100] Parenta[101] and Famly[102] all of which offer training, advice and support in this area.

REFLECTION FROM TRAINING – THANGALAKSHMI RAMAKRISHNAN

After sharing about developing a loving pedagogy in an online meeting, I was greatly encouraged when a practitioner shared her notes with me. I have asked permission to share them in this book:

Reflecting upon our practice in the light of a loving pedagogy will impact all areas of our provision, as these training notes demonstrate.

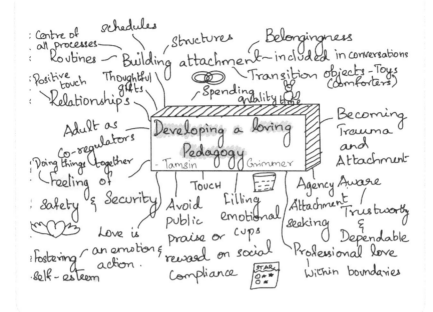

: Centre of   schedules
. all processes ——   structures   Belongingness
: Routines — Building attachment —— included in conversations
: Positive   Thoughtful   Transition objects - Toys
   touch   gifts   (comforters)
: Relationships   Spending
                                                  quality time

            Adult as ——   Becoming
           Co-regulators   Developing a loving   Trauma
: Doing things together   Pedagogy   and
   Feeling of   - Tamsin   Grimmer   Attachment
: Safety & Security   TOUCH   filling   Agency Aware
                                   Avoid   emotional   Attachment Trustworthy
                                   public cups   seeking   &
              Love is   praise or   Dependable
: Fostering an emotions   reward on social   Professional love
 Self-esteem action.   Compliance   STAR   within boundaries

Conclusion

Thank you for being brave and adopting a loving pedagogy. I hope this book has been useful and you have found it helpful to explore some of the terms relating to loving pedagogy in more detail. I also hope that you have reflected upon your practice as you have been reading this book. If you have any questions or comments or would like to share your loving pedagogy with others, please do get in touch.[96]

Your last task is to reflect upon your loving pedagogy and consider how you might explain and articulate it to others. Love is still a taboo subject for many within early childhood education, and we need to work together to ensure that loving our children is seen as the best and most appropriate way of nurturing them and supporting their learning and development. Let's talk about love at work, at home, on the bus, in the pub . . . everywhere! Together, we can ensure that love is given the priority it needs to help all children to flourish.

DOI: 10.4324/9781003510529-62

References

Introduction

1. Page, J. (2008) Permission to love them. In Nutbrown, C. and Page, J. (Eds), *Working with Babies and Young Children from Birth to Three*. London: Sage.
2. Page, J. (2011) Do mothers want professional carers to love their babies? *Journal of Early Childhood Research*, 9(3), 310–323.
3. Page, J. (2014) Developing 'professional love' in early childhood settings. In Harrison, L. and Sumsion, J. (Eds), *Lived Spaces of Infant-Toddler Education and Care – Exploring Diverse Perspectives on Theory, Research, Practice and Policy*. Volume 11. International Perspectives on Early Childhood Education and Development Series. London: Springer Publishing, pp. 119–130.
4. https://www.careforthefamily.org.uk/
5. https://5lovelanguages.com/
6. Chapman, G. and Campbell, R. (2012) *The 5 Love Languages of Children*. Chicago, IL: Northfield Publishing.
7. Maslow, A. (1943) A theory of human motivation. *Psychological Review*, 50(4), 370–396.
8. Grimmer, T. (2023) Is there a place for love in an early childhood setting? *Early Years*. DOI: 10.1080/09575146.2023.2182739
9. Grimmer, T. (2021) *Developing a Loving Pedagogy: How Love Fits with Professional Practice*. Abingdon: Routledge.

Part 1

10. UNICEF (1989) *United Nations Convention on the Rights of the Child.* www.unicef.org.uk/Documents/Publication-pdfs/UNCRC_PRESS200910web.pdf

11. Australian Children's Education and Care Quality Authority (2018) *Supporting Agency: Involving Children in Decision Making.* https://www.acecqa.gov.au/sites/default/files/2018-04/QA1_SupportingAgencyInvolvingChildreninDecisionMaking.pdf

12. Bowlby, J. (1953) *Childcare and the Growth of Love.* London: Penguin Books.

13. Ainsworth, M. and Bell, S. (1970) Attachment, exploration, and separation: Illustrated by the behavior of one-year-olds in a strange situation. *Child Development,* 41(1), 49–67.

14. Elfer, P. (2011) *Key Persons in Early Years Settings and Primary Schools.* London: Routledge.

15. Gerhardt, S. (2015) *Why Love Matters: How Affection Shapes a Baby's Brain.* 2nd edn. Hove: Routledge.

16. Main, M. and Solomon, J. (1986) Discovery of a new, insecure-disorganized/disoriented attachment pattern. In Brazelton, T. B. and Yogman, M. (Eds), *Affective Development in Infancy.* New York: Ablex.

17. Rose, J. and Rogers, S. (2012) *The Role of the Adult in Early Years Settings.* Maidenhead: Open University Press, p. 41.

18. Fisher, J. (2016) *Interacting or Interfering? Improving Interactions in the Early Years.* Maidenhead: Open University Press, p. 69.

19. Edwards, C., Gandini, L. and Forman, G. (2012) *The Hundred Languages of Children: The Reggio Emilia Experience in Transformation.* 3rd edn. Santa Barbara, CA: Praeger.

20. Clark, A. and Moss, P. (2017) *Listening to Young Children: A Guide to Understanding and Using the Mosaic Approach.* London: Jessica Kingsley Publishers.

21. Einarsdottir, J., Juutinen, J., Emilson, A., Ólafsdóttir, S., Zachrisen, B. and Meuser, S. (2022) Children's perspectives about belonging in educational settings in five European countries. *European Early Childhood Education Research Journal,* 30(3), 330–343.

22. Cyrus, M. (2023) *Flowers*. New York: Columbia Records.

23. Young, S. (2003) *Music with the Under Fours*. London: Routledge Falmer, p. 106.

24. Young, S. (2003) *Music with the Under Fours*. London: Routledge Falmer, p. 92.

25. March, K. and Young, S. (2006) Musical play. In McPherson, G. (Ed), *The Child as Musician*. Oxford: Oxford University Press, p. 290.

26. Hargreaves, D., Marshall, N. and North, A. (2003) Music education in the twenty first century: A psychological perspective. *British Journal of Music Education*, 20(2), 147–163.

27. Burke, N. (2013) *The Use of Recorded Music in Early Childhood Settings*. Birmingham, MA: Birmingham City University.

28. Grimmer, T. (2022) *Supporting Behaviour and Emotions in the Early Years: Strategies and Ideas for Early Years Educators*. Abingdon: Routledge.

29. Grimmer, T. and Geens, W. (2022) *Nurturing Self-Regulation in Early Childhood: Adopting an Ethos and Approach*. Abingdon: Routledge, pp. 203–204.

30. Noddings, N. (1992) *The Challenge to Care in Schools: An Alternative Approach to Education*. New York: Teachers College Press.

31. Strauss, C., Lever Taylor, B., Gu, J., Kuyken, W., Baer, R., Jones, F. and Cavanagh, K. (2016) What is compassion and how can we measure it? A review of definitions and measures. *Clinical Psychology Review*, 47, 15–27.

32. Edwards, C., Gandini, L. and Forman, G. (2012) *The Hundred Languages of Children: The Reggio Emilia Experience in Transformation*. 3rd edn. Santa Barbara, CA: Praeger, p. 170.

33. Department for Education (DfE) (2024) *Statutory Framework for the Early Years Foundation Stage*, p. 41. https://assets.publishing.service.gov.uk/media/65aa5e42ed27ca001327b2c7/EYFS_statutory_framework_for_group_and_school_based_providers.pdf

34. Department for Education (2022) *Health and Safety: Responsibilities and Duties for Schools*. Updated 5 April 2022. Crown Copyright. https://www.gov.uk/government/publications/health-and-safety-advice-for-schools/responsibilities-and-duties-for-schools

35. Wood, A. (2013) Is professional 'love' appropriate? *SecEd Blog*, 12 September. https://www.sec-ed.co.uk/content/blogs/is-professional-

love-appropriate/#:~:text=Given%20the%20practically%20 identical%20purposes,which%20underpins%20all%20effective%20 teaching

36. Gottman, J., Katz, L. and Hooven, C. (1996) Parental meta-emotion philosophy and the emotional life of families: Theoretical models and preliminary data. *Journal of Family Psychology*, 10(3), 243–268.

37. Gilbert, L., Gus, L. and Rose, J. (2021) *Emotion Coaching with Children and Young People in Schools*. London: Jessica Kingsley.

38. Reis, H. (2007) Propinquity. In Baumeister, R. and Vohs, K. (Eds), *Encyclopedia of Social Psychology*. Thousand Oaks: Sage.

39. Read, V. (2014) *Developing Attachment in Early Years Settings: Nurturing Secure Relationships from Birth to Five Years*. 2nd edn. Abingdon: Routledge, p. 59.

40. Read, V. (2014) *Developing Attachment in Early Years Settings: Nurturing Secure Relationships from Birth to Five Years*. 2nd edn. Abingdon: Routledge, p. 61.

41. Kuypers, L. (2011) *The Zones of Regulation*. Santa Clara, CA: Think Social Publishing Inc. https://www.zonesofregulation.com/index.html

42. Kingston-Hughes, B. (2024) *Why Children Need Joy: The Fundamental Truth About Childhood*. London: Sage.

43. Bedari Kindness Institute (2024) https://kindness.ucla.edu/

44. Sparks, A., Fessler, D. and Holbrook, C. (2019) Elevation, an emotion for prosocial contagion, is experienced more strongly by those with greater expectations of the cooperativeness of others. *PLOS One*, 14(12), e0226071.

45. Brooks, R. (2020) *The Trauma and Attachment Aware Classroom*. London: Jessica Kingsley.

46. Bradbury, A. and Grimmer, T. (2024) *Love and Nurture in the Early Years*. London: Sage, p. 1.

47. Bradbury, A. and Grimmer, T. (2024) *Love and Nurture in the Early Years*. London: Sage, p. 24.

48. Professional Love in Early Years Settings Project (undated) https:// www.eymatters.co.uk/wp-content/uploads/2021/04/pleys-report_ singlepages.pdf

49. Dr. Jools Page Research Profile. https://research.brighton.ac.uk/en/ persons/jools-page

50. University of West London (no date) *10 Ways to Be Respectful*. https://www. uwl.ac.uk/student-life/building-uwl-community/10-ways-be-respectful

51. Grimmer, T. (2022) *Supporting Behaviour and Emotions in the Early Years: Strategies and Ideas for Early Years Educators*. Abingdon: Routledge, p. 7.

52. Prevention of Cruelty to, and Protection of, Children Act 1889. https:// www.legislation.gov.uk/ukpga/1889/44/enacted

53. Byrne, J. (2016) Love in social care: Necessary pre-requisite or blurring of boundaries. *Scottish Journal of Residential Child Care*, 15(3), 152–158.

54. All-Party Parliamentary Group on a Fit and Healthy Childhood (APPG) (2020) *Wellbeing and Nurture: Physical and Emotional Security in Childhood*. https://fhcappg.org.uk/wp-content/uploads/2020/07/ReportWell beingandNurtureFinal140720.pdf

55. DfE (2023) *Working together to Safeguard Children*, p. 12. https:// assets.publishing.service.gov.uk/media/65803fe31c0c2a000d18cf40/ Working_together_to_safeguard_children_2023_-_statutory_guidance. pdf

56. Neff, K. (2024) *Definition of Self-Compassion*. https://self-compassion. org/the-three-elements-of-self-compassion-2/

57. Saltzberg, B. (2010) *Beautiful Oops*. New York: Workman Publishing Company.

58. Shanker, S., Hopkins, S. and Davidson, S. (2015) *Self-Regulation: A Discussion Paper for Goodstart Early Learning in Australia*. Peterborough, ON: The MEHRIT Centre Ltd.

59. Grimmer, T. and Geens, W. (2022) *Nurturing Self-Regulation in Early Childhood: Adopting an Ethos and Approach*. Abingdon: Routledge, p. 2.

60. Robson, D., Allen, M. and Howard, S. (2020) Self-regulation in childhood as a predictor of future outcomes: A meta-analytic review. *Psychological Bulletin*, 146(4), 324–354.

61. Vink, M., Gladwin, T. E., Geeraerts, S., Pas, P., Bos, D., Hofstee, M., Durston, S. and Vollebergh, W. (2020) Towards an integrated account of the development of self-regulation from a neurocognitive perspective: A framework for current and future longitudinal multimodal investigations. *Developmental Cognitive Neuroscience*, 45.

62. Eisenberg, N., Smith, C. and Spinrad, T. (2011) Effortful control – relations with emotion regulation, adjustment, and socialization in childhood. In

Vohs, K. and Baumeister, R. (Eds), *Handbook of Self-Regulation*. New York: Guilford Press, pp. 263–283.

63. Parten, M. (1932) Social participation among preschool children. *Journal of Abnormal & Social Psychology*, 27(3), 243–269.

64. Ferguson, S. (2022) *What Is a Warm Personality?* https://psychcentral.com/health/warm-personality#warm-personality-vs-warm-hearted-people

65. Harlow, H. F. (1958) The nature of love. *American Psychologist*, 13(12), 673–685.

66. Fiske, S., Cuddy, A. and Glick, P. (2007) Universal dimensions of social cognition: Warmth and competence. *Trends in Cognitive Science*, 11(2), 77–83.

67. Williams, L. and Bargh, J. (2008) Experiencing physical warmth promotes interpersonal warmth. *Science*, 322, 606–607.

68. Mainstone-Cotton, S. (2017) *Promoting Young Children's Emotional Health and Wellbeing: A Practical Guide for Professionals and Parents*. London: Jessica Kingsley Publishers, p. 10.

69. Mainstone-Cotton, S. (forthcoming) *Wellbeing Explained*. Abingdon: Routledge.

70. Read, V. (2014) *Developing Attachment in Early Years Settings: Nurturing Secure Relationships from Birth to Five Years*. 2nd edn. Abingdon: Routledge, p. 2.

71. Laevers, F. (2005) *Well-Being and Involvement in Care Settings: A Process-Oriented Self-Evaluation Instrument*. Leuven: Kind & Gezin and Research Centre for Experiential Education. https://emotionallyhealthyschools.org/wp-content/uploads/2020/09/sics-ziko-manual.pdf

72. The Children's Society (2015) *The Good Childhood Report*, p. 11. https://www.york.ac.uk/inst/spru/research/pdf/GCReport2015.pdf

Part 2

73. UNICEF (no date) https://www.unicef.org/child-rights-convention/convention-text-childrens-version

74. https://www.unicef.org/child-rights-convention

75. UNICEF (2002) *For Every Child*. London: Red Fox.

76. Holy Bible, New International Version (2011) https://www.biblegateway.com/passage/?search=1%20Corinthians%2013%3A4-8&version=NIV

77. Šaric, M. and Šteh, B. (2017) Critical reflection in the professional development of teachers: Challenges and possibilities. *Publication Center for Educational Policy Studies Journal*, 7(3), 67–86.

78. Pollard, A. and Tann, S. (1994) *Reflective Teaching in the Primary School*. 2nd edn. London: Cassell.

79. Schon, D. (1983) *The Reflective Practitioner: How Professionals Think in Action*. New York: Basic Books.

80. Dewey, J. (1910) *How We Think*. Lexington, MA: D.C. Heath.

81. Foong, L. and Nolan, A. (2018) Individual and collective reflection: Deepening early childhood pre-service teachers' reflective thinking during practicum. *Australasian Journal of Early Childhood*, 43(1), 43–51.

82. Rodd, J. (2013) *Leadership in Early Childhood: The Pathway to Professionalism*. Maidenhead: McGraw-Hill.

83. Bognar, B. and Krumes, I. (2017) Encouraging reflection and critical friendship in pre-service teacher education. *CEPS Journal*, 7(3), 87–112.

84. Bradbury, A. and Grimmer, T. (2024) *Love and Nurture in the Early Years*. London: Sage, p. 84.

85. Education Scotland (2020) *Realising the Ambition: Being Me*. https://education.gov.scot/media/3bjpr3wa/realisingtheambition.pdf

86. The Promise Scotland Ltd. (2020) *The Promise Scotland*. https://thepromise.scot

87. Malcolm, J. (2022) *Love, Policy and Professionalism: The Early Learning and Childcare Lead Professional*. Master of Philosophy Thesis. http://janeymphd.blogspot.com/2023/03/mphil-thesis-love-policy-and.html

88. Early Years Coalition (2021) *Birth to 5 Matters: Non-Statutory Guidance for the Early Years Foundation Stage*. St Albans: Early Education. https://birthto5matters.org.uk/wp-content/uploads/2021/04/Birthto5Matters-download.pdf

89. Music, G. (2017) *Nurturing Natures: Attachment and Children's Emotional, Sociocultural and Brain Development*. Abingdon: Routledge.

90. Zeedyk, S. (2013) *Sabre Tooth Tigers and Teddy Bears: The Connected Baby Guide to Understanding Attachment*. Dundee: Suzanne Zeedyk Ltd.

91. Siegel, D. and Bryson, T. (2020) *The Power of Showing Up: How Parental Presence Shapes Who Our Kids Become and How Their Brains get Wired*. London: Scribe.

92. Bowlby, J. (1969) *Attachment and Loss: Volume 1. Attachment*. New York: Basic Books.

93. Siraj, I., Kingston, D. and Melhuish, E. (2015) *Assessing Quality in Early Childhood Education and Care – Sustained Shared Thinking and Emotional Well-Being (SSTEW) Scale for 2–5-Year-Olds Provision*. London: Trentham Books.

94. Harms, T., Clifford, R. M. and Cryer, D. (1998) *Early Childhood Environment Rating Scale-Revised*. New York: Teachers College Press.

95. Harms, T., Cryer, D. and Clifford, R. M. (1990) *Infant/Toddler Environment Rating Scale*. New York: Teachers College Press.

96. Tamsin Grimmer's Website. https://www.tamsingrimmer.com/

97. Early Education. https://early-education.org.uk/

98. Early Excellence. https://training.earlyexcellence.com/w/uk/

99. Early Years TV. https://www.earlyyears.tv/

100. Kinderly. https://kinderly.co.uk/news-and-media/

101. Parenta. https://www.parenta.com/

102. Famly. https://www.famly.co/

Index

T - #0252 - 270225 - C182 - 210/148/8 - PB - 9781032836638 - Matt Lamination